ANTONIO
CARLUCCIO
PASSION FOR PASTA

SEDANI CON ZUCCHINI E NOCI
See page 151

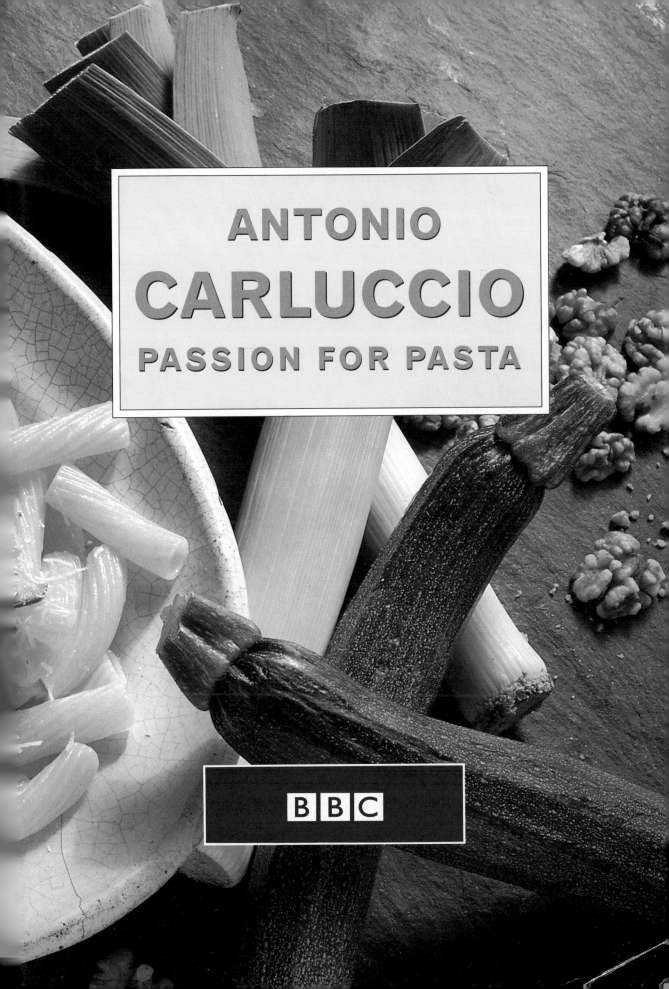

ANTONIO CARLUCCIO

PASSION FOR PASTA

BBC

ACKNOWLEDGEMENTS

Special thanks for their participation in producing this wonderful book to Heather Holden-Brown, Frank Phillips and Deborah Taylor of BBC Books; to Sylvie Wootton, for editing; to Chloe Cheese for having embellished my book with her illustrations; to Graham Kirk and Helen Payne for the marvellous photography and styling; to Caroline Robb for assisting me in testing the recipes; to Kate Webb and Judy Shawcross for typing and retyping; to Count and Countess Bernadotte and Gunilla and Richard Sutton for the suggestion of the recipe *Tullgarn's Pie*; and to Susan Fleming for updating this new edition.

To my mother and my wife Priscilla

PUBLISHED BY BBC WORLDWIDE LTD
Woodlands, 80 Wood Lane, London W12 0TT
First published in hardback 1993
Reprinted 1993 (twice), 1994
First published in paperback 1994
Reprinted 1994 (twice) 1995, 1996, 2000
This second, updated edition published 2003
Reprinted 2005, 2006

© Antonio Carluccio 1993, 2003

ISBN 0 563 36254 5 (Hardback)
ISBN 0 563 37059 9 (Paperback)
ISBN 0 563 48761 5 (Paperback second edition)

DESIGNED BY PETER BRIDGEWATER
ILLUSTRATIONS BY CHLOE CHEESE
STEP-BY-STEP DIAGRAMS BY ROB SHONE
PHOTOGRAPHS BY GRAHAM KIRK
STYLING BY HELEN PAYNE
FOR SECOND EDITION, REBECCA HARDIE
PRODUCTION CONTROLLER FOR SECOND EDITION, ARLENE ALEXANDER

Set in Berkeley Old Style by Keystroke, Jacaranda Lodge, Wolverhampton
Printed and bound in Great Britain by CPI Bath
Colour separations by Technik Ltd, Berkhamsted, Herts

CONTENTS

◆

INTRODUCTION

*T*HE everyday procedure in my family when I was a boy was to check on behalf of my mother if the trains were running on time so that she could throw the pasta into the boiling water. My father was a station master on the Italian railway and it was extremely important that the cooking of the fresh pasta coincided with his return for lunch as a family if we were all to enjoy a perfectly prepared dish. Being brought up like this, one naturally views a dish of pasta as something special, rather than just as a basic filler. Great attention and care were always given to the choice of ingredients for the sauce which varied daily and matched the type of pasta, hand-made or not, so producing many specialities.

When I went abroad as a student I took with me this knowledge and love of pasta, not knowing it would one day become the subject of my future profession. I remember seeing Italian films where entire families crowded round the kitchen table in the middle of which, next to the ever-present Chianti flask, was a huge pottery bowl full of steaming, freshly cooked pasta, just waiting to be assaulted and devoured with gusto by each member, young or old. Italy today is no longer like this. Pasta is still eaten at least once a day but more as a delicious part of a meal than as the staple diet. The 20 and more regions have provided such a variety of pasta specialities, always based on the best local ingredients, that it is impossible not to write a book about them.

In the north a few slices of the precious truffles may produce a wonderful result; while another delicious pasta dish will be achieved using some fresh sardines and wild fennel in Sicily; a tomato and basil sauce in Naples; and a pesto in Genoa. Wherever they are, Italians love pasta, and however it is served they know the trick is that it should never be overdressed with fancy sauces and complicated ingredients.

If you are still in any doubt as to why we Italians so enjoy preparing and eating one simple food, I will tell you. For me creating a pasta dish calls for the skills of a culinary artist; using a palette of delicious ingredients to produce a masterpiece of exquisite flavours and textures. I have devised the recipes in this book specially to inspire you so that you get as much enjoyment out of pasta. For now I would like you to forget about bottled sauces, ready-made pasta dishes, and pre-packed Parmesan cheese. Instead indulge yourself by trying the amazing soft texture of your own hand-made pasta, the bite of fresh Italian cheeses, the flavours of cured meats such as Parma ham, and anchovies and fresh basil. Certainly, too, I will have included a few of my two favourite ingredients, dried mushrooms and truffles!

Italians are fussy about the basic ingredients, but it isn't difficult to be as fussy yourself. Nearly all the recipes in this book use ingredients which are easy to find. More and more delicatessens and supermarkets are expanding their range of Italian-style ingredients. Because I am in no doubt as to how enthusiastic a pasta-lover you will become, I have included some very special recipes for dinner parties or bigger occasions. Even if some of the ingredients take a bit more effort to find, I know that once you have tried the finished dishes you will be pleased you have discovered them. In no time at all

you will have found your nearest supplier of dried mushrooms and truffles and be producing one of the more adventurous recipes.

I should tell you that once you have tried your hand at making fresh pasta it will be difficult to prevent yourself making it again, and again! You need nothing more than a little time to yourself – no fancy machinery, no enormous work surfaces. Alternatively a good brand of dried pasta can produce the most marvellous results and with such little effort.

Whilst the word pasta conjures up the warmth and hospitality of the Italian people, many believe that pasta was imported from China by the Venetian, Marco Polo. However, in the pasta museum in Rome (sponsored by the Agnesi family, one of the oldest producers of excellent dried pasta), there are some documents that record that a large tagliatelle-shaped pasta existed in Italy at least 20 years before Marco Polo returned from China. So we may never really be sure who can claim its origins.

If its history is slightly obscure, I can explain a little about the importance of pasta for each new generation. In Italy, like parents worldwide, we eagerly wait for a baby's first word: usually 'mamma' or 'papa'. But in Italy we also cherish the moment when a baby sucks on its first strand of spaghetti! All is well, a lifelong love of pasta lies ahead.

Italians don't only eat pasta, as some people like to believe, but it certainly represents, with all the endless varieties, a very important part of the daily diet. Every year, an Italian consumes the equivalent to 78 lb (35 kg) of pasta! In Britain the consumption is just over 7 lb (3 kg) per person, and it is on the increase. I think there is still plenty of room for improvement, but considering that the consumption is steadily increasing every year by approximately 20 per cent I feel reassured that pasta is winning the popularity it should.

I think it's almost time I let you read on to discover the pasta recipes for yourself. But first I need to tell you a little about the ingredients which make Italian food so good, and give you some quick tips on preparation. Once you have these basics nothing could be simpler than creating your own delicious pasta. During 40 or more years of loving to eat and cook pasta I have discovered many recipes which I am passing on to you in this book.

ANTONIO CARLUCCIO

La Pasta

·

PERFECT
PASTA

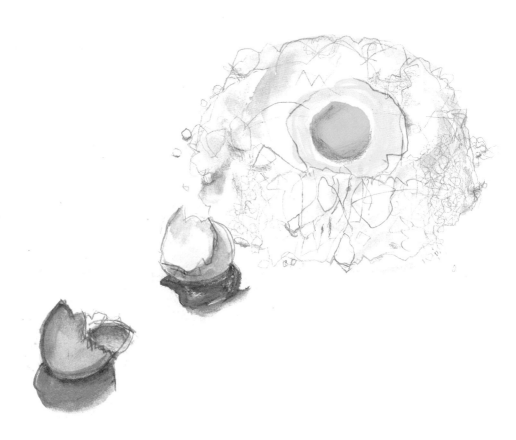

Take some wheat flour, add some water, work to a smooth dough, roll out, and cut into shapes, ribbons or strands. That's pasta! These days there are electronic machines, some of them over 100 yards long, which manufacture pasta, but they work with the very same ingredients. From milling the grain to drying and packaging the pasta, commercial equipment has automated the process to produce enough pasta to meet our enormous demands.

For commercial pasta there is one crucial ingredient, and that is durum wheat flour. Grown in limited areas of Europe, and imported from Canada and America, durum wheat grinds down into a form of hard semolina, which ensures that the pasta keeps its bite, and that it doesn't become soft and sticky when cooked. For hand-made pasta you need, however, 00 or double zero flour, a specially refined flour of tender wheat which, when combined with eggs, gives the necessary bite.

PASTA ITALIAN-STYLE

Whichever part of Italy you are in, you will find pasta combined with fresh, local produce, served alongside a salad and followed by fresh fruit. Often Italians eat a little pasta in between the antipasto and the fish or meat course.

We all know now that there is much more to learn from the Mediterranean style of cooking than we thought, especially in the south of Italy. There olive oil is used for most of the cooking, and pasta, vegetables and fruit are eaten in plenty, with little use of meat and animal produce. This diet has resulted in a lower incidence of coronary heart disease and related conditions.

There are plenty of ways of preparing pasta with sauces based on vegetables, and using olive oil instead of dairy products, and the results are delicious. None of the recipes in this book depends upon cream which, in my opinion, gives the same dairy taste to everything. However, there are certainly some treats to be enjoyed using fine Italian cheeses and cured meats.

Pasta itself is high in carbohydrate, and contains protein, vitamins and minerals. Its high carbohydrate content makes it one of the most popular foods for athletes, as it sustains their energy levels. Pasta with egg in it has a greater amount of protein, and the eggs give the pasta an extra bite. Incidentally, in America some manufacturers add extra vitamins to pasta to make it a 'superfood'. For me pasta is enough of a superfood as it is, and needs no modifying!

FRESH OR DRIED PASTA?

Fresh pasta reminds me of my childhood when my mother produced it as often as the bringing up of six children would allow. The table in the middle of our kitchen had a marble top; ideal for making pasta. In the centre my mother poured the wheat flour. I always thought this looked like Vesuvius covered with snow! She made the fresh pasta much the same way as I show you in this book, working every crumb of flour into the dough with a spatula until we had a bare and highly polished marble surface with a big, shiny ball of pasta on top. With her big wooden rolling pin, my mother flattened and transformed the dough into a large, thin sheet of pasta of immaculate texture and transparency.

Making the pasta dough looked messy at first but it was extremely sensual to mix the flour and eggs with our hands, when we were allowed to! Often, as children, our way of helping was to undo the little rolls of pasta strands and spread them on a clean, floured cloth, or to detach the little squares of ravioli from each other which she made for special occasions.

A plate of freshly made pasta is a real delicacy, but to earn this compliment it has to be produced with the kind of care my mother gave it, which I will tell you about later.

I am never very sure about recommending anyone to buy fresh pasta unless they can trust the person producing and selling it commercially. Fresh pasta has been known to contain a lot of water in order to increase its weight! In fact I have never seen the quantities of eggs and flour displayed on fresh pasta, nor have I seen any indication of how fresh it really is. Usually you can't tell whether you have bought good or poor-quality fresh pasta until you get it home. A poor-quality one will swell considerably during cooking, absorbing a lot of water, and is likely to become a sticky mass.

However, dried pasta can taste heavenly too, if it is well prepared, and accompanied by the right sauce. Dried pasta is available with or without eggs, and if you get a good brand you can be sure of its consistent quality. At least if you buy dried pasta it should have a 'sell by' date. I am not an expert on all the brands but I particularly recommend De Cecco or Buitoni or Agnesi or Voiello. An artisan producer also makes some pastas under my name to my own specifications. Sometimes I prefer to use dried pasta anyway because of the huge variety of shapes that it offers.

EQUIPMENT

You don't have to have any special equipment to make your pasta, and I am not a fan of electric pasta machines in the home. The simplest hand machines will help you, but everything can be done by hand perfectly well. A pastry cutting wheel will be useful for some of the shapes. Specialist shops often sell ravioli wheels which will do instead, or buy a raviolatrice which is like a rectangular grid that cuts through the dough to make the ravioli. Make sure you have a rolling pin.

You do need a large steel saucepan for cooking the pasta, and a large colander. A few of the recipes ask you to cook the sauce for quite a time, so check that your saucepan has a heavy enough base to stand up to this length of cooking!

PASTA SHAPES

I would understand it if you felt manufacturers of pasta purposely confused us all with the different names they give to each pasta shape. Altogether, Italians have invented more than 300 different shapes of pasta, each one suitable for a certain sauce. So it is not so surprising that they are not always labelled by the same name commercially. But don't be put off by the choice – the variety makes for so much fun.

The shape of pasta is more important than you may think. The pleasure of eating the right combination of texture, shape and flavour is taken very seriously. One of

CAPELLI D'ANGELO

ORECCHIETTE

MACCHERONCINI

SPAGHETTINI

SPAGHETTI/VERMICELLI

GOMITI

SEDANINI

SPAGHETTONI

LINGUE DI PASSERO

LINGUINE

TRENETTE

RIGATONI

BUCATINI

LASAGNE RICCIA

PIZZOCCHERI

TUBETTI

GNOCCHETTI SARDI

FUSILLI

TUBETTINI

TORTIGLIONI

PENNETTE

CANNELLONI

MARILLE

PENNE

ORECCHIONI ROSSI

ORECCHIONI VERDI

CONCHIGLIE

the companies, Voiello, even commissioned a car designer, Giugiaro, to come up with a technically perfect shape of pasta, not for its aerodynamics, but so it would collect as much sauce as possible to make each morsel succulent and delicious. The car designer's peculiar construction was a short tube, ridged inside, with wings! The pasta, unfortunately out of production now, was called marille. Generally speaking, anything with the word rigate after it is ridged, and anything called lisce is smooth.

'Pasta corta' SHORT PASTA •

Short pasta covers everything from the tiny decorative shapes that go into soups, to the fancy bows, shells and tubular pastas which are served with different sauces.

'Pasta lunga' LONG PASTA •

What is called spaghetti in one region is called vermicelli in another, but long pasta describes the long, string-like noodle, which can be as fine as 'angel's hair', or as thick as spaghettoni. There are flat versions of long pasta too, like the well-known lasagne.

'Pasta ripiena' FILLED PASTA •

Italians have created envelopes of pasta containing delicious fillings in many shapes and sizes. Every Italian family has a favourite pasta filling which varies greatly from southern to northern Italy. It is worthwhile making filled pasta because it is so satisfying. You can really test your skills when making this pasta and although you may find agnolotti, raviolini, tortellini and cappelletti in ready-made dried form, these will take longer to cook.

• HOW MUCH PASTA? •

Pasta makes a good main course, or a starter. My general advice is that for a starter $3^{1}/_{2}$ oz (90 g) dried pasta or $4^{1}/_{2}$ oz (120 g) fresh pasta per person is more than sufficient.

If it is eaten as the main course and accompanied by a salad, with a dessert to follow, you need 4–$4^{1}/_{2}$ oz (100–120 g) dried pasta per person or $4^{1}/_{2}$–5 oz (120–150 g) fresh pasta, depending on appetite and on the quality and shapes.

COOK IT RIGHT

•

Most of the miserable disasters served in dubious restaurants are due to three faults: the first being the use of bad-quality pasta; secondly, that the pasta has been precooked and then reheated; or thirdly, that it's been badly cooked in the first place. It is vital, and imperative, to cook the pasta *just* before serving it, and to follow these golden rules.

Cooking times for different pasta shapes

PASTA	FRESH	DRIED	SHAPE
Agnolotti	5	8	F
Anolini	3/4	8	F
Brandelli	3/4		S
Bucatini		7/8	L
Cannelloni	4	10/12	L
Cappellacci	6	12	F
Cappelletti	7	12	S/F
Capelli d'angelo	1/2	3/5	L
Conchiglie		7/8	S
Farfalle	1/2	8/9	S
Festoni		8/9	L
Fettuccine	5/7	10/12	L
Fidelini		7/8	L
Fusilli		8/9	S/L
Gnocchetti sardi		10/12	S
Gomiti		7/9	S
Lasagne	4/5	10/12	L
Lingue di passero		7/10	L
Linguine		8/10	L
Maccheroncini		7/8	L
Maltagliati	4/5		S
Marille		10/12	S
Orecchiette	6	12/15	S
Orecchiette baresi		10/12	S
Orecchioni		20/25	S
Pappardelle	5/7	7/8	L/S
Penne/tte lisce	1/2	5/8	S
Penne rigate	1/2	7/8	S
Pizzoccheri		20/25	L
Ravioli	1/2		F
Ravioloni	5		F
Rigatoni		8/9	S
Sedani		8/9	S
Spaghetti/Spaghetti alla chitarra	3/5	8	L
Spaghettini	3/4	5/6	L
Tagliatelle	3/5	5/6	L
Taglierini	1	4/5	L
Tagliolini	1/2	4/5	L
Tajarin	1/2	4/5	L
Tortelli	5/10		F
Tortellini	5/6	8	F
Tortelloni	4/5		F
Tortiglioni		6/7	L
Trenette		8/10	L
Tubetti lisci		8/9	S
Tubettini		7/8	S
Vermicelli	4	7/8	L
Zita/Zite/Ziti		7/9	L

S Short L Long F Filled

LASAGNE

SPAGHETTI QUADRATI

ORECCHIETTE

RAVIOLINI

TORTELLINI

TAGLIATELLE/FETTUCCINE

BRANDELLI

ANOLINI

PAPPARDELLE

CAPELLI D'ANGELO AL NERO DI SEPPIA

TAGLIOLINI DI PORCINI

FETTUCCINE ALLA SEPPIA

TAGLIATELLE ALLA BIETOLA

MALTAGLIATI

FESTONI

RAVIOLONI

FARFALLE

CAPPELLACCI VERDI

THE SAUCEPAN •

Has to be big enough to contain abundant water; ideally it should be shaped so it is large at the bottom to keep the temperature of the water constant. You will need a lid to cover the saucepan briefly after you have immersed the pasta, in order to bring the water quickly to boiling point again. After the water has come back to the boil remove the lid for the remaining cooking time.

THE WATER •

Should be boiling when the pasta goes in. You really do need plenty of water, for example 1¾ pints (1 litre) of water per 4 oz (100 g) of dried pasta, because whilst the pasta is absorbing water, it is losing starch, and you don't want it to reabsorb the starch because the water is saturated with it.

You can also try using fresh chicken stock (see page 36) to cook especially fine lengths or small shapes of pasta: they will taste much better. In fact when we use pasta with a soup broth, the pasta is usually cooked in the broth itself.

THE SALT •

Has to be added just before the pasta. Use coarse sea salt if possible and in the ratio of ½ oz (10 g) of salt per 1¾ pints (1 litre) of water.

OIL •

It is only necessary to add oil to the cooking water when you cook large, flat pieces of pasta such as lasagne. For this you immerse the pasta pieces, one by one, so the swimming oil coats the surface of the lasagne and prevents the pieces sticking together.

For all the other pasta shapes you simply have to stir frequently at the beginning of the cooking time (using a wooden fork) to keep the pasta separated. Then, just remember to stir again, from time to time, during the remaining cooking.

THE AL DENTE TEST •

Italians are careful about the way pasta is cooked, with good reason. Pasta is cooked until it is al dente when, although cooked, it still has some bite to it, which is just how it should be. But al dente means different things to different people, and you will find it best to taste a piece of pasta regularly as you are cooking it to get it just as you like it. Neapolitans tend to eat spaghetti with so much bite that the strands uncurl and spring off the plate! However, with the guidance on cooking times on page 17 you will pass the al dente pasta test without any problems.

DRAINING •

This is where you need a large colander. When the pan of pasta is taken off the heat I suggest you add a little cold water to stop the cooking process; and then drain the pasta.

Never try to rinse the drained pasta under cold water or indeed hot water – you will take away the precious starch coating.

Make sure you always save a little of the cooking water: it's often the best way to moisten the pasta if it is too dry or 'loosen' the sauce if it becomes too thick.

Once the pasta is drained put it back into the saucepan, or straight into a pre-heated dish. This helps keep the pasta warm whilst you add a dressing.

DRESSING PASTA ◆

Some people sprinkle their cooked pasta with olive oil, or put a few knobs of butter on it before dressing it with a sauce, but I suggest you add a little of the cooking water. Then add some of the sauce and toss the pasta to coat each piece. Finally, serve it on warm plates, pour more sauce over the top, and sprinkle with freshly ground black pepper, and some freshly grated Parmesan or Pecorino cheese, or herbs as required.

◆ EASY EATING ◆

Two basic rules for eating pasta properly are almost constantly broken. The first is you don't need both a spoon and a fork to collect long pasta. (The spoon is best kept for soup, or the very small pasta shapes.) To eat spaghetti like an Italian, lift a little pasta and sauce on to your fork, make a small space on the side of the plate, and turn the fork like a screwdriver, collecting the spaghetti on to it. Whatever you do, try not to suck in long pieces of spaghetti which are dangling off the fork. You'll spray sauce everywhere.

The second rule is much harder to keep! The rule is not to use a piece of bread to collect the sauce on the plate – but I love to break this rule if the sauce is irresistible!

SAUCES

◆

This is very much in the hands of the cook because as you will see there are a thousand possibilities. The choice of ingredients is as much influenced by personal taste as by what is available. Generally speaking, the better the person's sense of taste, the better the sauce. A few basic rules help, though.

The first rule is to combine the right sauce with the right type of pasta. Never make outrageous combinations: they never taste good!

The second rule is that pasta should never swim in a sauce. The quantities of sauce to pasta should be such that only an irrelevant amount of sauce remains on the plate after you have eaten the pasta.

The third rule is to dress the pasta immediately after it has been cooked, by tossing it with the sauce just before serving and adding a little extra sauce over the top.

La Dispensa

THE ITALIAN LARDER

The Italian larder, la dispensa as it is known in Italian, is carefully stocked with a few essentials for producing pasta at any time. With a well-equipped larder, as suggested here, you will be all set to be both creative and spontaneous!

FLOUR

When durum (or hard) wheat is first ground it produces a semolina, which is the main ingredient for making commercially produced pasta. You can buy durum flour in good Italian delicatessens. It keeps for some time provided you store it in an airtight jar or container.

Double zero flour, otherwise known as farina 00, is tender wheat specially refined for using in the most delicate, hand-made egg pasta. (It is also used in Italian cakes.) Sometimes it will help to use a mixture of durum flour and farina 00 to produce certain types of pasta. You can use ordinary plain flour but the softer result will not be as authentic.

TOMATOES

First made their appearance in Italy towards the end of the sixteenth century, but it was around 1900 that a Neapolitan company started one of Italy's main exports – by producing tinned tomatoes. Of all the regional cookery, Neapolitan still makes the most use of the wonderful flavour of local tomatoes.

In Britain the best way to reproduce the exceptional flavour of fresh Italian tomatoes is to use those in tins, cartons or bottles, because you almost never come across those fleshy, sweet-smelling tomatoes which have ripened under the Italian sun. Not for nothing are Italian tomatoes given the name pomodoro, meaning golden apple! I know some people add sugar to try to compensate for under-ripe tomatoes. It never works very well.

At home in southern Italy, we preserve our precious tomatoes in special, wide-necked bottles. The tomatoes are peeled and sealed in sterilised bottles, with some basil. They are really delicious.

In the last twenty years the Italian food industry has made it much easier for you to get quality tomatoes in many different forms – in cans, in cartons, in tubes and in jars. The best products come from Naples, Salerno or Parma, the three main areas for tomatoes in Italy. Try to keep one item from each of the following groups in stock.

PEELED PLUM TOMATOES •
Whole or chopped, usually sold in tins in their own juice but also in jars.

CREAMED AND PULPED TOMATOES •
Known as passata di pomodoro (usually in cartons or bottles) and polpa di pomodoro, slightly coarser.

Tinned plum tomatoes provide more liquid than creamed or pulped tomatoes, because these last two alternatives have had most of the excess water removed, along with the seeds. This means that if you substitute creamed or pulped tomatoes for whole or chopped tinned tomatoes, you can cut down on the cooking time because you don't need to evaporate so much liquid.

TOMATO PURÉE OR PASTE •
Usually sold in tins or tubes and in various concentrations but also in a block called Estratto. Sun-dried tomatoes and sun-dried tomato paste are two very special ingredients indeed, which I would also encourage you to look for. You can find them in delicatessens or shops specialising in Italian foods and in most supermarkets.

Tomato purée or paste is a must in the larder. What a pity that the triple or even six-times concentrate of tomatoes is not readily available here; it is so good you can even spread it on toast with some olive oil for a very tasty snack.

READY-MADE SAUCES

Although they are the quickest way to prepare a meal I would not suggest keeping them in stock. (Although, if necessary, there are some good varieties – Carluccio's, for example!)

OILS AND BUTTER

Olive oil has been used for the past 2000 years by Italians in the south of the country. (In northern Italy they more often use butter.) In the last decade or so, however, with the discovery that olive oil is better for your health, various types of this oil have been produced. For myself, I wouldn't dream of using any vegetable oil other than olive oil; but I do use butter for special occasions.

EXTRA VIRGIN OLIVE OIL •
This is very green, sometimes cloudy, and has a strong taste. It is the extract of the first pressing of olives. It has very little acidity, and its unique flavour is only good on salads or cold dishes; it is rarely used for cooking, but can be used as flavouring for cooked pastas and soups.

VIRGIN OLIVE OIL •
Is a little more refined than the previous type but for similar use and usually cheaper.

PASTA E PISELLI (left)
See page 40
ZUPPA DI TAGLIOLINI E POLLO (right)
See page 41

'PURE' OLIVE OIL ✦

Has been more refined and this is the most commonly used oil in Italy. A good-quality product will have a fine flavour, without being overpowering for cooking purposes. And it is the cheapest of all three types!

BUTTER AND LARD ✦

Butter is used in cooking mainly from central Italy upwards and across all of northern Italy. It is used to make the white sauces which accompany the pasta. In the region of Emilia Romagna the famous cucina bolognese uses large quantities of butter.

Lard is still used as a cooking fat in the south. The fat from the pig is preserved by salting and air-drying and then is sliced, cubed and rendered. This lardo is often the basis of meat sauces such as a battuto (with other flavourings). The crisp little morsels left are cioccioli, the Italian equivalent of pork scratchings, and are used in breads.

PANCETTA AND SPECK

Pancetta is the Italian equivalent of bacon and is used a great deal in Italy in the same way streaky bacon is used here. It comes in two shapes, rolled or flat, and has been air-cured with the addition of some spices. It is used in various sauces but even so I suggest you buy it in slices rather than the whole roll. If you can't find pancetta you can use bacon.

Guanciale is used in Lazio instead of pancetta, especially for the famous carbonara sauce. It is cured and air-dried cheeks of pork.

Speck is of Austrian origin and has always been used in the border regions of Trentino Alto Adige where many recipes include this very tasty, air-dried and smoked pork. It is very popular throughout Italy because although it is rather similar to Parma ham it costs much less and is extremely delicious. You can buy speck in every good delicatessen and I suggest you get a small piece which you can keep for a long time in the fridge. Alternatively, substitute smoked bacon.

PARMA HAM

Perhaps surprisingly it is the fat of Parma ham which is particularly useful for sauces and soups. You may find you can buy just the end of a Parma ham from your delicatessen. It will be cheaper than buying slices from the main part and very useful when fried in small cubes to add flavour to a sauce or soup.

TUNA FISH AND ANCHOVIES

A couple of tins or jars of good tuna fish in oil and anchovy fillets in jars or tins are essential for some of the sauces based on fish. The best anchovies are whole ones preserved in salt from delicatessens. They give the best flavour, but if you can't get these use tinned anchovies, filleted in oil. Before you use salted anchovies soak them in water for 30 minutes to lessen their saltiness. Pat them dry on paper towels and remove any large bones before using them. To preserve them further, put them in a bowl and cover with olive oil.

OLIVES AND CAPERS

Usually black olives are used in typical Sicilian sauces, along with small capers. Choose capers which are preserved in salt and not in vinegar or brine, if possible. They are increasingly available now and they keep well. Soak them for 30 minutes in water before straining and using them.

CHEESES

In Italy we say 'Come il cacio sui maccheroni' ('Like cheese on pasta') to describe two things which are so appropriate together they become virtually inseparable. Pasta without a sprinkle of freshly grated Parmesan cheese is almost unthinkable. There are, however, dishes where cheese is taboo, such as when pasta has a fish sauce, or the famous Aglio e olio e peperoncino with its chilli flavouring.

PARMESAN •
Only cheese made in the region of Reggio Emilia is able to carry the name Parmigiano reggiano (the full, registered Italian name for Parmesan). It is made with cows' milk and its fat content is low (only 30 per cent), but it has a particularly fine smell and taste. It should have a very grainy texture, without smelling 'cheesy' at all. It is usually at least 14 months old, pale yellow and comes in huge sizes of about 50–60 lb (22.5–27 kg). Buy a tiny wedge of it, which, wrapped in aluminium foil, will keep in the refrigerator for several weeks. There is also a fresh Parmesan-type cheese which has matured for just 10 months. This is fine eaten in pieces, but it is unsuitable for grating.

There are some other similar cheeses, such as Grana padano which is made in the Po Valley, but it is not renowned for being as good as Parmigiano reggiano. You can tell the quality of the Parmesan from what it does in soups and sauces. If it melts, and becomes lumpy on the bottom of the plate, it is not such a good-quality cheese.

Whatever you do, try to use a piece of fresh Parmesan and grate it yourself. Drums and sachets of ready-grated Parmesan will positively spoil a dish.

PECORINO •

The three best-known versions of this sheep's milk cheese come from the regions of Lazio (Pecorino Romano), Sardinia (Pecorino Sardo), and Tuscany (Pecorino Toscano). Pecorinos are also found in Sicily, Calabria, Puglia and Campania. Throughout southern Italy Pecorino is often used in place of Parmesan cheese. It is a quick-maturing cheese and is excellent fresh and grated.

Known as Pecorino da grattugiare, a mature Pecorino is almost as hard as Parmesan cheese in texture, and gives certain recipes an extra 'bite'.

RICOTTA •

This is a low-fat, soft cheese, similar to cottage cheese, but is not at all sour. In fact when ricotta has any hint of acidity, it is 'off'. It can be made from goats', sheep's or cows' milk (the cows' milk variety is most readily available here). Ricotta is mostly used in filled pasta such as cannelloni or tortellini or ravioli.

There is also a matured version of ricotta cheese which is suitable for grating. Made from either sheep's or goats' milk, it is very hard and salty, and called ricotta salata.

FONTINA •

Fontina is a semi-soft cheese exclusive to the Val d'Aosta region in the Alps where the herds of cows graze on the sweet, alpine grass all summer long. No wonder the result is a deliciously sweet, melting cheese, which is pale cream with a red rind. It is classed as a table cheese, but is also used for cooking. Be sure it is the real version and not an imitation.

MOZZARELLA •

The tastiest Mozzarella is that which has been traditionally made from buffaloes' milk. It is a soft cheese made by working the curd by hand while it is very hot to obtain a spongy, milky-textured ball. You'll find it sold in a plastic bag or container in its own whey, but it has to be used straight away. In good delicatessens you can get smoked Mozzarella too. Either use Mozzarella as the filling in pasta timbales or enjoy it sliced raw with tomatoes.

MASCARPONE •

I would hardly call mascarpone a cheese although it still belongs in this category. It is like a very smooth and sweet, thickened double cream. It is a very fresh, unfermented cheese made from cows' milk and usually sold in cartons.

Because of its creaminess we eat it not only as a table cheese but also use it in the famous Tiramisù dessert, and as a dessert in its own right, sprinkled with sugar!

HERBS AND SEASONINGS

BASIL •

Is without doubt the king of the herbs in Italian cookery. It originally came from India, via Arabia, to the south of Italy; enthusiasm for its use spread over the rest of Europe, and now basil is one of the most favoured herbs. Only fresh basil leaves produce that wonderful, sweet scent we all know. The dried ones taste completely different. Nowadays it is possible to grow basil through the winter too, so there need not be any temptation to use the dried variety.

If you can't get fresh basil, however, the famous Pesto alla Genovese may be the solution. Pesto is a sauce originally made from a very small-leafed variety of basil, grown along the Ligurian Riviera (see Trenette al pesto, page 132).

PARSLEY •

This is also widely used in pasta dishes. The flat-leafed form, often known as Continental parsley, has a more concentrated smell and flavour. Parsley is at its best used fresh; when dried it does not have any flavour at all.

BAY LEAVES, ROSEMARY, OREGANO, MARJORAM AND SAGE •

These five herbs are all-important in Italian cookery and although I always prefer to use them fresh, I admit that the dried varieties still have a natural aroma when cooked.

SALT •

It helps to have salt in two forms – coarse and fine – and it should be sea salt.

PEPPER •

I only keep whole black peppercorns because freshly ground pepper tastes infinitely better than the ready-ground sort. Fresh green peppercorns are not as highly flavoured as the dried ones, and are used in some Italian dishes.

CHILLI •

I once bought some bunches of chillies from New Covent Garden market to decorate my restaurant. I thought they looked very innocent with their green, yellow, orange and red colours. But tasting one of them I discovered that not even in India had I ever tasted anything more lethally pungent and piercing! Be very careful with the use of chilli and remember that the green variety is not any less hot. Having said all this, it's not a bad idea to keep some chillies on a string in the larder as they retain much of their flavour when dried. This spice is used almost exclusively in the south, especially in Calabria where they call it diavolilli, little devils.

GARLIC, ONIONS AND SHALLOTS

Rather than swallow garlic pills as a natural remedy Italians make good use of the bulb itself. It is widely used for flavouring sauces of many sorts. Because it keeps well you should always have some hanging in the kitchen. If you are allergic or very sensitive to garlic then steep some garlic cloves in a bottle containing olive oil, and use the garlic-flavoured oil rather than the cloves themselves. But don't keep the garlic in oil for a long time. Olive oil is not a preserving agent.

Both onions and shallots are widely used, with the shallot offering a compromise between garlic and onion. The large Spanish onions tend to be milder in flavour than the smaller, white-skinned variety. In some recipes porri (leeks) are also used. The sweetest red onion of Italy is undoubtedly the Tropea type from Calabria. It can be eaten raw almost like an apple!

DRIED MUSHROOMS

So beloved are dried wild mushrooms to me that I keep many varieties in my larder, and I would encourage you to keep at least ceps and morels.

All dried mushrooms need to soak before they are used. Leave them in warm water for 20 minutes. Drain them and squeeze the mushrooms dry. Strain and keep the soaking liquid because it comes in useful for moistening sauces. Just watch that the grit that collects at the bottom of the soaking bowl doesn't get through the strainer.

CEPS •

In Italy we call cep mushrooms porcini, and in France they call them cèpes. They are possibly the most common of the dried mushrooms, although not the cheapest. I use them mainly in winter when the choice of fresh wild mushrooms is limited.

Ceps have a very distinctive, concentrated flavour, almost like meat extract, so it is enough to use dried ceps in small quantities. They improve the flavour of sauces considerably, and if you add a few dried cep mushrooms whenever you use ordinary fresh mushrooms you will be pleased with the resultant richer flavour. Just 1 oz (25 g) dried ceps will make all the difference to 1 lb (450 g) fresh mushrooms.

Dried ceps are usually sold sliced in packets. They are quite expensive so treat them with great care and store them in an airtight container once you have opened the packet (or in the freezer).

MORELS •

Only very specialised shops sell the most expensive wild mushroom, the morel, that grows profusely in parts of Tibet, Kashmir and Nepal in springtime. The dried morel has a very intense flavour, almost like bacon. It is usually only available whole.

When it's been soaked in water, the dried morel regains most of its original shape and texture. Because of this slices of morel make a very pretty garnish.

FRESH MUSHROOMS

The most commonly available mushrooms are the cultivated relatives of the field mushroom, *Agaricus campestris*. They are fairly bland in flavour, but button, open-cap or flat mushrooms can be useful in the kitchen. Try some of the many exotic mushrooms now cultivated, among them shiitake and oysters. To give freshness and that certain 'je ne sais quoi' to some sauces, introduce these exotic species to your cooking, possibly adding a small quantity of dried ceps for extra flavour.

But fresh wild mushrooms are still the best. Ceps, morels and chanterelles only grow in the wild. The seasons for buying them are springtime for morels and chanterelles, and August to late autumn for ceps. These fresh varieties are very expensive so you can't afford to experiment with them, and I suggest you follow a recipe rather than improvising.

TRUFFLES AND TRUFFLE OIL

The only form in which to use truffle for me is fresh. This very expensive commodity is available only between October and January. Naturally I am talking about the white truffle from around Alba in Piedmont. It reaches its very high prices because it is so much sought after and the demand is huge. Truffle is a fungus that grows under the earth and can't be cultivated. If you want a real treat, then buy a small one. A ¹/₂ oz (10 g) serving per person is sufficient.

The black truffle, which can also be partially cultivated, is found in Umbria in Italy and in Périgord in France. It is used mainly for cooking but is not intense enough to flavour the whole dish. A combination of fresh black truffle and some truffle oil could be a life-saver in some situations.

Truffle oil of good quality is the next best thing to a fresh truffle, but only to give a slight flavour to some dishes.

Minestre e Salse Semplici

SOUPS AND
SIMPLE SAUCES

The variety of soups in Italy is practically endless. Each family produces soups to suit their taste, using ingredients according to their availability, but always creating some fantastic results from what is to hand.

Soup is very much part of the Italian evening meal, especially when it is followed by a light main course. Italians sometimes serve a well-flavoured consommé between courses, or

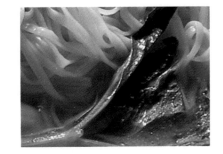

prepare a more substantial minestrone for lunch or the evening meal – especially in winter.

When you add pasta to soup you can enjoy the texture of the pasta along with all the other flavours – and it is quite different from eating pasta with a sauce. But rather than my keep telling you, why not make the soups I have created here so you can enjoy them for yourself?

In this chapter I have also included some very basic sauces, which you will be able to return to time and time again. They are made with just a few ingredients, such as oil, onions or garlic, tomatoes and herbs. Once again, in spite of their simplicity it is imperative that the best ingredients are used in order to achieve the perfect result.

Brodo di pollo

CHICKEN STOCK

To produce a wonderful chicken stock use a 'boiler' chicken, preferably a free-range one. If you haven't a large enough saucepan to get the bird in whole, then cut it into portions before you start. Chicken stock can also be produced using the cheaper cuts of chicken like legs, wings, etc. Home-made chicken stock is so useful it is worth cooking plenty in advance and freezing it in batches. You can also eat the cooked chicken meat, of course.

MAKES ABOUT 5½ PINTS (3 LITRES)

4 lb (1.75 kg) chicken or chicken pieces
Bouquet garni or a sprig of parsley and a bay leaf
7 pints (3.9 litres) water
1 large onion, peeled and quartered
3 carrots, peeled and quartered
3 celery sticks (with leaves if possible)
Salt
Few black peppercorns

METHOD

Put all the ingredients in a large pan and bring to the boil. Gently skim off the scum as it rises to the surface using a large flat spoon. Reduce the heat, cover and simmer for at least 2 hours. Remove the chicken. Strain the stock and discard everything else. Once the stock has gone cold remove any solidified fat.

Pastina in brodo

SOUP WITH PASTA

This is the simplest of all soups – it is very much used in northern Italy, especially for the evening meal when it is warming but not too heavy. It is based on very good, home-made chicken stock. Do not use stock cubes to hurry the process.

♦

2 pints (1.2 litres) chicken stock (see opposite)
1 ripe tomato, peeled, de-seeded and finely chopped
5 oz (150 g) dried capelli d'angelo
Salt
1 oz (25 g) freshly grated Parmesan cheese
2 teaspoons finely chopped chives

♦

METHOD

Bring the stock to the boil, add the tomato and cook for a few minutes. Add the pasta and cook for another 3–5 minutes. Taste and add salt if necessary. Serve hot sprinkled with the Parmesan cheese and chives.

VARIATION

Cappelletti in brodo

SOUP WITH CAPPELLETTI

You'll find it easier to use dried pasta for this recipe, rather than making your own. However, if you do decide to make your own (see page 48) or you manage to find some fresh cappelletti or raviolini in a shop, use 9 oz (250 g) and cook it for 5–7 minutes.

2 pints (1.2 litres) chicken stock (see opposite)
1 ripe tomato, peeled, de-seeded and finely chopped
5 oz (150 g) cappelletti or raviolini
Salt
1 oz (25 g) freshly grated Parmesan cheese
2 teaspoons coarsely chopped celery or
a few leaves flat-leaf parsley

♦

METHOD

Follow the method in Pastina in brodo (see above), allowing the pasta 7–12 minutes to cook. Serve hot sprinkled with the Parmesan cheese, and either the celery or the parsley.

Minestrone

MINESTRONE

There are many different varieties of minestrone, each one varying according to regional customs. Minestrone ('big soup') is usually prepared with leftover fresh vegetables such as peas, shredded cabbage and courgettes. I'll allow you to substitute a stock cube for home-made stock in this recipe, but only if you really have to! Depending on quantities and proportions of ingredients, minestrone can also be served as a main course. This soup makes an excellent vegetarian recipe if the meat is left out.

SERVES 4

3 tablespoons olive oil
1 onion, peeled and chopped
1 small clove garlic, peeled and chopped
2 rashers streaky bacon, rinded and finely chopped, or
1 oz (25 g) Parma ham, finely chopped (optional)
4 celery sticks, diced
1 tomato, peeled, de-seeded and finely chopped
1 large carrot, peeled and diced
2 potatoes, peeled and diced
Few leaves fresh basil, or 1 tablespoon pesto sauce (see Trenette al
pesto, page 132)
1$\frac{1}{2}$ pints (900 ml) chicken stock (see page 36)
Salt
Freshly ground black pepper
1 × 13 oz (375 g) tin borlotti beans, drained
4 oz (100 g) dried tubettini
3 oz (75 g) freshly grated Parmesan cheese

METHOD

Heat the oil and fry the onion and garlic, with the chopped bacon or Parma ham (if using), until the onion is soft. Add the remaining vegetables, the basil or pesto, and toss well with the oil. Add the stock and bring to the boil. Cook for 10 minutes. Add salt and pepper to taste and stir in the borlotti beans and the pasta. Cook for about 10 minutes, or until the pasta is al dente. Serve hot sprinkled with the Parmesan cheese.

Pasta e fagioli

PASTA E FAGIOLI

This is my own version of a peasant soup which is also enjoyed in some of the best restaurants all over Italy. For this dish, the Neapolitans use pasta called munnezzaglia which is all the leftovers from different packets of pasta. (Break larger pieces of pasta into smaller bits.) If the recipe originates from Naples it will contain cannellini beans; if it's from other parts of Italy you'll find it has borlotti beans instead. To quicken the preparation of this dish I suggest using tinned beans instead of dried.

◆

SERVES 4

2 tablespoons olive oil
2 cloves garlic, peeled and finely chopped
1 carrot, peeled and diced
2 potatoes, peeled and diced
1 celery stick, diced
1 large tomato, peeled, de-seeded and diced
2 pints (1.2 litres) chicken stock (see page 36)
2 × 13 oz (375 g) tins cannellini or borlotti beans, drained
7 oz (200 g) munnezzaglia, or dried tubettini
1 small chilli pepper, finely chopped
2 basil leaves, shredded
Salt
Freshly ground black pepper
1 tablespoon virgin olive oil

◆

METHOD

Heat the oil and sweat the garlic. Add the vegetables and toss well. Pour in the stock, bring to the boil and simmer for 5 minutes.

Add half the beans. Mash the remaining beans to a pulp with the back of a fork and add to the stock with the pasta, the chilli and the basil. Cook gently for another 8 minutes, stirring from time to time to prevent the mixture sticking.

Serve with a trickle of virgin olive oil on top.

Pasta e piselli

PASTA WITH PEAS

This dish was made by my mother as soon as the very tender and sweet, new season peas were available; it can also be made with very fresh broad beans. She used to make a plain pasta, from just flour and water, purposely for this dish so that when cooked it had a marvellously soft texture. I suggest you use a large and possibly flat type of eggless pasta and cook it a little longer than usual so that you achieve the same softness. Don't use tinned peas for this recipe; if you can't find fresh peas then use frozen ones.

◆

SERVES 4

3 tablespoons olive oil

1 small onion, peeled and finely sliced

2 oz (50 g) cooked ham, cut into very thin strips

11 oz (300 g) podded fresh garden peas (or broad beans)

2 pints (1.2 litres) chicken stock (see page 36)

7 oz (200 g) dried lasagne or pappardelle, broken into pieces

6 basil leaves, chopped

Salt

Freshly ground black pepper

◆

METHOD

Heat the oil and fry the onion until soft, then add the ham, the peas and the stock and cook for 10 minutes or until the peas are soft.

Add the pasta and the basil, taste and add salt and pepper, and cook for another 10 minutes until the pasta is soft.

Zuppa di tagliolini e pollo

CHICKEN SOUP WITH TAGLIOLINI

One doesn't need to be a gastronomic genius to create a recipe like this, but, as often happens, by experimenting and testing one recipe, another comes out as a by-product. The result was so remarkable with this experiment that I had to include it in this book!

After I tested a recipe based on chicken breast, I put the rest of the chicken including the wing in water to be boiled for the cat. I went to the garden, collected a few leaves of lovage, a herb similar in flavour to celery but much more scented, and a handful of flat-leaf parsley. I cheated a little by adding a chicken stock cube but the revelation was the lovage, which gave so much flavour to the stock that it had to be discarded after a short part of the cooking time. With the addition of the pieces of boiled chicken I, not the cat, had a wonderful meal!

SERVES 4

1 lb (450 g) chicken bones, with some meat on them

2$^{1}/_{2}$ pints (1.5 litres) water

1 chicken stock cube

5 oz (150 g) dried tagliolini or 9 oz (250 g) fresh tagliolini
(see pages 48–50)

2 lovage leaves

Salt

3 oz (75 g) freshly grated Parmesan cheese

2 tablespoons chopped flat-leaf parsley

METHOD

Put the chicken bones and the water in a large pan with the stock cube, cover and simmer for 1 hour. (You can do this in advance.) Remove the bones, strain the stock, and cut the cooked meat off the bones and into small slivers. Discard the bones.

Return the stock to a clean pan, bring to the boil, add the pasta, the lovage and the chicken slivers. Allow to simmer for 2 minutes, then discard the lovage. Check and continue cooking the pasta until soft, and add salt if necessary.

Serve sprinkled with the Parmesan cheese and parsley. Because of the difficulty of eating this dish, the usually forbidden act of using a fork and spoon is allowed!

TAGLIOLINI PRIMAVERA
See page 57

Sugo di pomodoro

TOMATO SAUCE

There are many ways to make a tomato sauce. This is a very basic and quick version, but it makes an excellent standby when hunger beats the clock!

◆

SERVES 4

1 oz (25 g) butter or 2 tablespoons olive oil
1 large onion, peeled and finely chopped
1 × 14 oz (400 g) tin chopped tomatoes
6 basil leaves, chopped
Salt
Freshly ground black pepper

◆

METHOD

Heat the butter or oil in a pan and fry the onion until soft. Add the tomatoes and cook gently for 10 minutes. Stir in the basil, season with salt and pepper, and cook for another 5 minutes.

VARIATION

◆

Here's a very simple variation to make.

1 celery stick, finely chopped
1 tablespoon chopped parsley
1 clove garlic, peeled and finely chopped

◆

METHOD

Add the above ingredients when frying the onion in the Sugo di pomodoro recipe (above) and continue as before.

Ragù Bolognese

◆

BOLOGNESE SAUCE

Another indispensable recipe. Although it takes some time to cook this sauce the actual preparation is very easy and it is very tasty. The best result is achieved by using a piece of pork and a piece of lamb, both on the bone, but any combination, or all of one meat, will do.

The result is a deliciously condensed sauce which we would eat with our pasta, to be followed by the meat as a main course. If you want the meat to serve 4 as a main course increase it to 2¼ lb (1 kg) all told.

◆

SERVES 4

1 oz (25 g) butter or 2 tablespoons olive oil
1 large onion, peeled and finely chopped
10 oz (275 g) lamb, beef or pork with bone
¼ pint (150 ml) red wine
2 × 14 oz (400 g) tins chopped tomatoes
6 basil leaves, chopped
Salt
Freshly ground black pepper

◆

METHOD

Heat the butter or oil in a heavy-based pan and fry the onion until soft. Add the meat and fry for several minutes until browned. Add the wine and continue cooking for 2–3 minutes. Stir in the tomatoes, cover and simmer very gently for 1½ hours. Stir the contents from time to time. If the sauce becomes too dry add a little water.

When the sauce has been simmered for 1½ hours add the basil, salt and pepper, and cook uncovered for another 30 minutes.

Pasta Fresca

FRESH PASTA

I have specially chosen the sauces in this chapter because they go so well with the texture of fresh pasta. Whether you make your own pasta or buy it fresh will depend on how much time you have. Making your own pasta will probably take you about 30 minutes for the actual preparation, but you will get quicker with practice! If you buy fresh pasta you will have to accept that neither the quality nor freshness may match that of your own hand-made pasta.

You can make enough of your own pasta to store some. Cut the pasta into whatever shapes you want, leave it to dry completely on a clean tea towel, then pack it very carefully in an airtight bag or container. It is worth winding long strands,

such as tagliatelle, into nests while the pasta is still pliable to help protect them. The pasta will keep in the refrigerator for 2–3 days or in the freezer for a couple of months.

Finally, if you do decide to buy dried egg pasta instead of using the fresh egg pasta suggested here check the cooking times on page 17. Generally speaking, dried pasta takes about twice the cooking time allowed for fresh. You will usually find the dried egg pasta comes in nest shapes packed in transparent cellophane bags or boxes.

Pasta all'uovo

FRESH PASTA

This is where you can experiment using different flours (see page 24). I think Italian 00 flour (farina 00 or doppio zero) is the easiest to work with by hand. You could make up the weight with a little semolina flour. A small, hand-operated machine can be useful, but making pasta by hand is still one of the best ways. This recipe is for egg pasta.

◆

MAKES ABOUT 1 LB (450 G)

11 oz (300 g) Italian 00 flour
3 medium eggs
Pinch of salt

◆

METHOD

Sift the flour on to a work surface (marble is ideal), forming it into a volcano-shaped mound with a well in the centre. Break the eggs into the well and add the salt. Incorporate the eggs into the flour with your hands, gradually drawing the flour into the egg mixture until it forms a coarse paste. Add a little more flour if the mixture is too soft or sticky and with a spatula scrape up any pieces of dough. Before kneading the dough clean your hands and the work surface. Lightly flour the work surface, and start to knead with the heel of one hand. Work the dough for 10–15 minutes until the consistency is smooth and elastic. Wrap the dough in cling film or foil and allow it to rest for half an hour.

Again, lightly flour your work surface, and a rolling pin. Gently roll the dough out, rotating it in quarter turns to a sheet ⅛ inch (3 mm) in thickness. If you are making filled pasta go straight ahead and incorporate the filling as in the recipes (see pages 82–105). If you are making flat pasta or shapes leave the pasta on a clean tea towel to dry for about half an hour.

VARIATIONS

When you add one of the following colourings you may need to increase the proportion of flour to eggs slightly so that your mixture doesn't become too wet.

PASTA VERDE ◆ GREEN PASTA
Add 3 oz (75 g) well-drained, puréed cooked spinach to the basic ingredients.

Add 4 tablespoons beetroot juice to just 2 eggs when making the dough. (You will need a juicer or food processor to extract the beetroot juice.)

PASTA ROSSA ◆ RED PASTA

Add 1½ tablespoons tomato purée to the basic ingredients.

PASTA NERI ◆ BLACK PASTA

Add 1 teaspoon cuttlefish ink to the basic ingredients.

MAKING PASTA

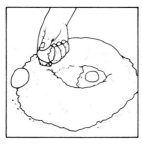

1 *The eggs are broken into a well in the centre of the flour. If you want coloured pasta add the relevant ingredient at this point.*

2 *Mix the eggs and flour together and, when all the ingredients are incorporated, knead the dough thoroughly.*

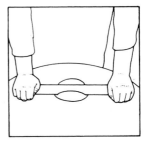

3 *Using plenty of flour to avoid sticking, begin rolling the ball of dough.*

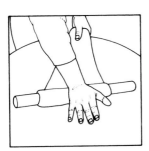

4 *As the pasta is rolled out it should be gently stretched using the rolling pin to pull the dough evenly.*

5 *To keep the dough from sticking and to help keep the thickness of the dough even, it should be turned regularly.*

6 *After rolling the dough on to the rolling pin replace it on the work surface on its reverse side.*

◆ LONG PASTA ◆

Long pasta shapes are probably the best known of all – spaghetti and lasagne are standard ingredients in most storecupboards.

The easiest way to make the long and delicate shapes such as capelli d'angelo, tagliolini, fettuccine and spaghetti alla chitarra is with a machine. But you can still successfully make some of the long shapes by hand and it is probably faster because there is less washing up! See the photographs on pages 14–15 and 18–19 for guides to how different kinds of long pasta look.

The best way to store long pasta is in a nest to avoid breaking the long strands.

Fold the sheet of pasta dough into a wide, flat sausage.

PAPPARDELLE: *Cut the rolled pasta into* 3/4 *inch (2 cm) strips.*

TAGLIATELLE: *Cut the rolled pasta into* 1/4 *inch (5 mm) strips.*

TAGLIOLINI: *Cut the roll of pasta into* 1/8 *inch (3 mm) strips.*

Shake out the strips of pasta and then, holding the pasta at one end, wind it into a nest to dry.

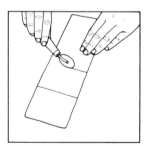

LASAGNE: *Cut a trimmed oblong of pasta into large squares and stack, separated with greaseproof paper, to dry.*

◆ FILLED PASTA ◆

Filled pasta may look difficult and fiddly to make, but, on the contrary, it is remarkably easy – and really delicious too. There's no comparison between the home-made and shop-bought varieties. You can also experiment with different fillings to make sumptuous and very impressive party pieces.

The basic shapes for making filled pasta are few, but simply by making them in different sizes you can achieve some interesting variations. The pasta shapes shown below are a guide for your own experiments. See the photograph on pages 18–19 for details of differing sizes of filled pasta shapes.

RAVIOLI: *Cut out two equally sized pieces of pasta dough 14¹/2 × 9¹/2 inches (37 × 24 cm). Dot evenly with filling. Moisten with egg to aid sealing.*

2 *Place the second piece of pasta over the first, pressing down around the filling to push out the air.*

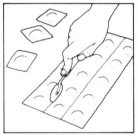

3 *Divide the ravioli into separate pieces using a serrated pastry wheel.*

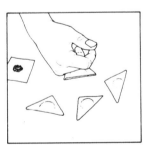

CAPPELLACCI: *Fill small 1 inch (2.5 cm) squares of pasta, fold into a triangle, pushing out all the air around the filling and pressing the edges to seal.*

2 *Bring the two widest points of the triangle together, pinching them firmly so they hold. Turn the pointed end of the triangle up at an angle to complete the shape.*

CANNELLONI: *Take a long strip of trimmed pasta dough. Roll up the filling in the pasta. Moisten the overlapping edges and trim.*

• SHORT PASTA •

Short pasta includes shapes such as farfalle (butterflies) and garganelli, which are made from flat dough, but also shapes such as orecchiette (ears) and gnocchetti sardi made by shaping balls of pasta with your fingers. Garganelli, which can be made by hand, is a good substitute for penne, which can only be made by machine. The very simplest short pasta shape, gnocchi, is made from simply slicing a sausage-like length of pasta dough. See the photographs on pages 14–15 and 18–19 for details of how other short pasta shapes look. To make any short pasta shape ribbed, simply roll it against a butter-pat or other similar ridged surface.

It makes for a very enjoyable half-hour to sit and sip a glass of wine and create delightful pasta shapes.

1 *Start with a rolled-out piece of pasta dough.*

2 *Trim the edges of the pasta dough with a serrated wheel. Divide the dough into two oblongs roughly 4 × 16 inches (12 × 36 cm).*

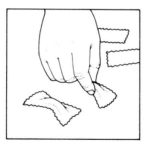

3 *Next, divide the two oblongs into neat squares of pasta of approximately 2 × 2 inches (6 × 6 cm).*

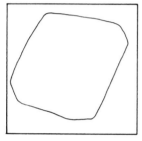

FARFALLE: *Divide your squares into halves to form oblongs using a serrated pastry wheel.*

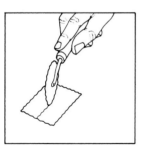

2 *To form the bow or butterfly shape pinch the oblong of dough in the centre.*

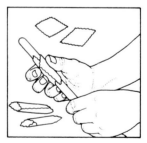

GARGANELLI: *Take a 2 inch (6 cm) square of pasta, moisten one side with water and roll firmly, and at a slight angle, around the end of a wooden spoon. Then roll over a ridged butter-pat.*

FUSILLI: *Cut the 2 inch (6 cm) square into four long strips.*

2 *Firmly roll a strip of pasta on to a knitting needle to form a spiral. Take out the needle and leave the fusilli to dry.*

BRANDELLI: *The simplest pasta shape ever – just tear a piece of rolled dough at random to form uneven pieces.*

ORECCHIETTE: *Roll out a piece of dough into a sausage shape of around 1/2 inch (1 cm) in diameter and 12 inches (30 cm) in length.*

2 *Cut the length of dough into small 1/2 inch (1 cm) pieces, then roll to form an even ball.*

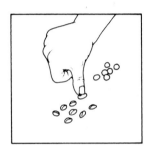

3 *To make the orecchiette press on the ball of dough, at the same time pushing it away from you slightly so that the dough curls into a shell, or ear, shape.*

GNOCCHETTI: *Make a small sausage of pasta of about 1 inch (2.5 cm) in length.*

2 *Press the pasta on to a ridged butter-pat. Press and push it firmly to form a small ridged sausage.*

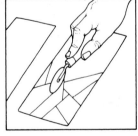

MALTAGLIATI: *Take a large oblong of pasta and cut it arbitrarily using a plain pastry wheel.*

TAGLIATELLE AI FEGATINI
See page 68

Capelli d'angelo al limone

ANGEL'S HAIR WITH LEMON

An extremely delicate fresh pasta such as this deserves a delicate sauce. Capelli d'angelo is practically the finest cut of pasta you can obtain either by machine or by hand. It cooks in less than a minute, so when you put the pasta on to cook make sure everyone is ready to eat it!

◆

SERVES 4

2 oz (50 g) unsalted butter
3 tablespoons double cream, with a little milk if necessary
Finely grated rind and juice of ½ lemon
1 lb (450 g) fresh capelli d'angelo (see pages 48–50)
2 oz (50 g) freshly grated Parmesan cheese
Salt
Freshly ground black pepper
Sprigs of parsley

◆

METHOD

Gently melt the butter and then, over a very low heat, stir in the cream and the grated lemon rind.

In a separate pan cook the pasta for just under 1 minute or until al dente, then drain, and add it to the sauce. Sprinkle with the lemon juice and Parmesan cheese, and add salt and pepper to taste. Toss well and distribute on to warm plates. Garnish each serving with a sprig of parsley.

Tagliolini primavera

♦

SPRINGTIME TAGLIOLINI

This is my own variation on the famous pesto sauce. It is a lovely dish to greet springtime with, when the desire for the fresh taste of herbs seems to intensify.

Try to cook the sauce by substituting, omitting or adding different herbs to suit your personal taste – it doesn't matter – but include at least five. Rather than blend all the herbs to a fine paste I prefer to chop everything very finely by hand to give a little texture to the sauce.

If you want to substitute dried pasta for the fresh choose lingue di passero.

♦

SERVES 4

3 oz (75 g) butter
1 clove garlic, peeled and very finely chopped
8 tablespoons finely chopped mixed fresh herbs, e.g. basil, mint,
coriander, dill, chervil, parsley, chives
1 tablespoon finely chopped sage, or rosemary, or oregano
1 oz (25 g) shelled hazelnuts, toasted
Finely grated rind of $\frac{1}{2}$ lemon
3 oz (75 g) freshly grated Parmesan cheese
4 tablespoons virgin olive oil
Salt
Freshly ground black pepper
1 lb (450 g) fresh tagliolini (see pages 48–50)

♦

METHOD

Melt the butter, add the garlic and gently heat it through – do not fry it. Add the herbs, hazelnuts, lemon rind and half the Parmesan cheese. Now stir in the olive oil, salt and pepper.

Meanwhile, cook the pasta for 1 minute or until al dente, drain and toss it in the sauce. Add a little of the cooking water if the mixture is too dry. Serve sprinkled with the remaining Parmesan cheese.

TAGLIATELLE AL RADICCHIO E RUCOLA
See page 65

Tagliolini con vitello

TAGLIOLINI WITH VEAL

This is a more substantial dish in which the veal can be replaced by chicken breast for a similar, but cheaper, dish. It is an almost instant meal because the meat cooks in such a short time.

◆

SERVES 4

9 oz (250 g) lean veal
6 tablespoons olive oil
1 onion, peeled and finely chopped
3 tablespoons dry white wine
8 leaves fresh sage, roughly chopped
Salt
Freshly ground black pepper
1 lb (450 g) fresh tagliolini (see pages 48–50)
3 oz (75 g) freshly grated Parmesan cheese

◆

METHOD

Cut the meat into very fine strips. Heat the oil and fry the onion until transparent. Add the meat and fry for about 5–7 minutes until browned and cooked through. Pour in the wine and let it evaporate for 1–2 minutes. Add the sage, and salt and pepper to taste.

Meanwhile, cook the pasta for 1–2 minutes or until al dente. Drain the pasta and reserve 1 tablespoon of cooking water to moisten the sauce. Stir the pasta into the sauce with the reserved water, and heat through. Sprinkle with the Parmesan cheese and toss well.

Tajarin al burro e tartufo

TAJARIN WITH BUTTER AND TRUFFLE

This is perhaps the quickest and easiest pasta recipe of all, but I am afraid it is also the most expensive! Truffle, especially the white variety from Alba, is one of the most sought-after delicacies, and one of the dearest.

It is almost unnecessary to say that to celebrate the most appreciated and sophisticated dish from Piedmont, where I come from, it is absolutely essential to have freshly made tagliolini or tajarin as they are called there.

◆

SERVES 4

1 lb (450 g) fresh tagliolini (see pages 48–50)
2 oz (50 g) unsalted butter, roughly chopped
3 tablespoons double cream
Salt
Freshly ground black pepper
3 oz (75 g) freshly grated Parmesan cheese
2–2$\frac{1}{2}$ oz (50–65 g) white Alba truffle, very finely sliced

◆

METHOD

Cook the pasta for 1–2 minutes or until al dente. Drain and reserve a little of the cooking water. Toss the pasta in the butter until every strand is coated. Add the cream, salt and pepper, and enough of the reserved water to achieve a smooth consistency. Sprinkle with the Parmesan cheese and toss well. Serve with the fine slices of truffle on top of each portion.

SPAGHETTI QUADRATI ALLA BAGNA CAUDA
See page 71

Tagliatelle verdi con prataioli

TAGLIATELLE VERDI WITH FIELD MUSHROOMS

This recipe is especially dedicated to all those mushroom gatherers who safely collect the well-known field variety, Agaricus bisporus, *which is found growing wild in Britain, and is related to the cultivated button mushroom. Naturally this dish tastes better with the wild, field variety, but you can substitute the cultivated one. To make the result interesting I use green pasta.*

SERVES 4

6 tablespoons olive oil
2 cloves garlic, peeled and finely sliced
11 oz (300 g) field or button mushrooms, roughly sliced
4 tablespoons dry white wine
4 oz (100 g) speck with fat, rinded and cut into strips
Salt
Freshly ground black pepper
1 lb (450 g) fresh green tagliatelle (see pages 48–50)
3 oz (75 g) freshly grated Parmesan cheese
4 tablespoons finely chopped parsley

METHOD

Heat the oil and sweat the garlic. Add the mushrooms and fry them over a low heat to extract their moisture. Pour in the wine and let it evaporate for 1–2 minutes. Add the speck, and salt and pepper to taste.

Meanwhile, cook the pasta for 3–5 minutes or until al dente. Drain the pasta, and toss in the sauce. Serve sprinkled with the Parmesan cheese and parsley.

Tagliatelle al radicchio e rucola

TAGLIATELLE WITH RADICCHIO AND ROCKET

The bitterness and the sharpness of rocket gives a quite sophisticated taste to this pasta, which, when combined with the speck, reminds me of the style of cooking in north-east Italy.

•

SERVES 4

4 tablespoons olive oil
1 red onion, peeled and roughly chopped
4 oz (100 g) speck, rinded and cut into small strips
2 tablespoons dry red wine
5 oz (150 g) radicchio, finely chopped
Salt
Freshly ground black pepper
1 lb (450 g) fresh tagliatelle (see pages 48–50)
4 oz (100 g) rocket, roughly chopped

•

METHOD

Heat the oil and gently fry the onion and the speck, until the onion is soft. Pour in the wine and let it evaporate for 1–2 minutes. Now add the radicchio, and allow it to soften. Add salt and pepper.

Meanwhile, cook the pasta for 3–5 minutes or until al dente. Drain and mix with the sauce. Serve sprinkled with the chopped rocket.

PAPPARDELLE CON SELVAGGINA E PORCINI
See page 76

Tagliatelle ai fegatini

TAGLIATELLE WITH CHICKEN LIVERS

Chicken livers are very much part of many Italian sauces, and in this dish they predominate. Extremely easy to prepare, this is a particularly tasty recipe.

◆

SERVES 4

11 oz (300 g) chicken livers, trimmed
6 tablespoons olive oil
1 large onion, peeled and very finely sliced
4 bay leaves
Pinch of nutmeg
3 tablespoons dry sherry
2 tablespoons tomato purée
About 2 tablespoons stock or water
Salt
Freshly ground black pepper
1 lb (450 g) fresh tagliatelle (see pages 48–50)
3 oz (75 g) freshly grated Pecorino cheese

◆

METHOD

Cut the chicken livers into small slivers. Heat the oil and fry the onion very gently for 5 minutes. Add the chicken livers and bay leaves, and fry gently for another 6 minutes over a low heat.

Add the nutmeg and sherry, and let the alcohol evaporate for 1–2 minutes. Stir in the tomato purée, and enough stock or water to bring the sauce to a smooth consistency. Add salt and pepper to taste.

Meanwhile, cook the pasta for 3–5 minutes or until al dente. Drain and toss well in the sauce. Serve sprinkled with the Pecorino cheese.

Tagliatelle alla bottarga

·

TAGLIATELLE WITH BOTTARGA

This Sardinian speciality, not well known here in England, is based on bottarga, which is salted and air-dried roe of grey mullet or tuna fish. Bottarga is usually grated over pasta as a flavouring, but can also be eaten in thin slices with lemon and oil as an appetiser. The best bottarga for this recipe is the tuna. It is an extremely quick recipe provided you can get hold of the bottarga. It is not impossible to find it here, but you'll need the help of a good Italian delicatessen! There is a pre-grated variety in jars which gives quite good results.

◆

SERVES 4

4 tablespoons virgin olive oil
1 medium onion, peeled and finely chopped
1 lb (450 g) fresh tagliatelle or spaghetti (see pages 48–50)
Salt
1 tablespoon chopped parsley
1 tablespoon chopped basil
2 oz (50 g) bottarga, grated

◆

METHOD

Heat the oil and fry the onion until transparent.

Meanwhile, cook the pasta for 3–5 minutes or until al dente, adding only a little salt to the cooking water as the bottarga is itself very salty. Drain the pasta and toss in the olive oil and onion. Add the chopped parsley and basil, and the grated bottarga.

Paglia e fieno con zucchini e Pecorino

'STRAW AND HAY' WITH COURGETTES AND PECORINO

My version of straw and hay is nothing else than white and green fresh tagliolini cooked together. Many sauces go well with this combination of pasta. Here is one which is simple and tasty at the same time.

◆

SERVES 4

2 tablespoons olive oil
2 oz (50 g) butter
1 onion, peeled and finely chopped
1 clove garlic, peeled and finely chopped
14 oz (400 g) firm courgettes, cut into matchsticks
2 ripe tomatoes, sliced into small segments
5 basil leaves, chopped
8 oz (225 g) each of white and green fresh tagliolini
(see pages 48–50)
Freshly ground black pepper
Salt
3 oz (75 g) freshly grated Pecorino cheese

◆

METHOD

Heat the oil and butter, and gently fry the onion and garlic. Add the courgettes with the tomatoes, and continue to fry gently, stirring, until cooked. This takes a good 10–12 minutes. Add the basil.

Meanwhile, cook the pasta for 1 minute or until al dente and drain. Mix the pasta with the sauce. Add some freshly ground black pepper and salt to taste. Serve with plenty of Pecorino cheese.

Spaghetti quadrati alla bagna cauda

SQUARE SPAGHETTI WITH GARLIC AND ANCHOVY

This is a recipe of which I am very proud. It is along the lines of bagna cauda, that famous garlic and anchovy sauce from Piedmont which is usually eaten as part of an antipasto. The sweetness of the grilled red and yellow peppers contrasts perfectly with the garlic and anchovy. This type of pasta is also called maccheroni alla chitarra because it is made using a stringed cutter which resembles a guitar.

SERVES 4

2 whole bulbs garlic, peeled and broken into cloves
10 fl oz (300 ml) milk
16 anchovy fillets (salted or in oil)
3 peppers (yellow and red)
3 oz (75 g) butter, roughly chopped
1 lb (450 g) fresh square spaghetti (see pages 48–50)

METHOD

Cook the garlic cloves gently in the milk for approximately ½ hour until softened. If using salted anchovies soak them in water for ½ hour. Dry the anchovies on paper towels and remove any large bones. Meanwhile, put the peppers under a hot grill until the skins are blackened. Allow to cool slightly, then peel the skin away from the peppers, discard the seeds, and finely slice them. Keep the pepper slices warm.

When the garlic is soft take the pan off the heat. Add the anchovies and stir with a spoon until dissolved. Pass the milk, garlic and the anchovies through a metal sieve into a pan. Heat gently and add the butter. Do not cook the sauce, just heat it enough to melt the butter. Take the sauce off the heat.

Meanwhile, cook the pasta for 3–5 minutes or until al dente. Drain and toss well with the sauce. Serve the pasta with the slices of pepper on top.

Fettuccine verdi al sugo dinoci

FETTUCCINE VERDI WITH WALNUT SAUCE

From the region of Liguria in the north, this sauce makes good use of the area's local ingredients. It goes well with flat pasta, pasta shapes and even served on filled pasta. Fettuccine is the wider version of tagliatelle and is very popular in Rome.

SERVES 4

1 tablespoon fresh white breadcrumbs
5 oz (150 g) shelled walnuts or hazelnuts
1 small clove garlic, peeled
2 oz (50 g) freshly grated Pecorino cheese
Salt
1 tablespoon chopped marjoram
6 tablespoons virgin olive oil
4 tablespoons strained Greek yoghurt
1 lb (450 g) fresh green fettuccine (see pages 48–50)
Freshly ground black pepper

METHOD

Soak the breadcrumbs in water for 10 minutes, then squeeze them dry.

Meanwhile, immerse the walnuts or hazelnuts in hot water and try to remove as much of their brown skins as you can. Dry them on paper towels. Put the walnuts or hazelnuts in a mortar together with the breadcrumbs, the garlic, the Pecorino, salt and marjoram. Pound the ingredients with a pestle to a fine texture. Transfer the mixture to a small bowl. Slowly add the oil, stirring constantly with a spoon. Finally, stir in the yoghurt to make a smooth sauce.

Meanwhile, cook the pasta for 5–7 minutes or until al dente. Drain the pasta and toss with the sauce. Serve with plenty of freshly ground black pepper.

Pappardelle al sugo di carne

PAPPARDELLE WITH MEAT SAUCE

Pappardelle is a very satisfying pasta indeed, especially when it is accompanied by a meat sauce. This pasta is eaten in Italy whenever a roast is made, with the meat sediment from the roasting tin forming the basis of the sauce. In this recipe I have given you a quicker version.

◆

SERVES 4

6 tablespoons olive oil

1 small onion, peeled and finely chopped

1 celery stick, finely chopped

1 carrot, peeled and finely chopped

7 oz (200 g) minced pork (or use skinned 100% pork sausages)

7 oz (200 g) lean minced beef

1/4 pint (150 ml) dry red wine

3 tablespoons tomato purée diluted with 2 tablespoons warm water

2 bay leaves

1/4 pint (150 ml) stock

Salt

Freshly ground black pepper

1 lb (450 g) fresh pappardelle (see pages 48–50)

3 oz (75 g) freshly grated Parmesan cheese

◆

METHOD

Heat the oil and gently fry the onion, celery and carrot until soft. Add the pork and beef, and continue frying until the meat is browned. Pour in the wine and let it evaporate for 1–2 minutes. Add the tomato purée with the water, and the bay leaves. Cook for another 10 minutes.

Stir in the stock, add salt and pepper to taste, and heat through for 1–2 minutes. Remove the bay leaves.

Meanwhile, cook the pasta for 5–7 minutes or until al dente. Drain and serve with the meat sauce, and sprinkle with the Parmesan cheese.

BRANDELLI AI CARCIOFI
See page 79

Pappardelle con selvaggina e porcini

PAPPARDELLE WITH GAME AND CEPS

Hare is the sort of game Italians would combine with this pasta, and for me game and wild mushrooms are inseparable. So long as you make up the same overall quantity of game you can combine any two or three choices from the following: rabbit, hare, pheasant, partridge, venison, grouse, wild duck, or wood pigeon. Because the sauce takes a little longer than others to make we'll call this a Sunday dish!

◆

SERVES 6

1 oz (25 g) dried ceps or 7 oz (200 g) fresh ceps
6 tablespoons olive oil
1 large carrot, peeled and finely chopped
2 celery sticks, finely chopped
1 large onion, peeled and finely chopped
1 clove garlic, peeled and finely chopped
8 oz (225 g) boneless rabbit meat, coarsely chopped
8 oz (225 g) boneless breast of wood pigeon or pheasant, or fillet of venison,
coarsely chopped
$^{1}/_{4}$ pint (150 ml) dry red wine
2 bay leaves
1 × 1 lb (450 g) carton or bottle creamed or pulped tomatoes
Salt
Freshly ground black pepper
$1^{1}/_{4}$ lb (550 g) fresh pappardelle (see pages 48–50)
3 oz (75 g) freshly grated Parmesan cheese

◆

METHOD

If using dried ceps, soak them in warm water for 20 minutes.

Heat the oil and fry the carrot, celery and onion for 1–2 minutes. Add the garlic and fry for another minute. If using fresh mushrooms, finely slice them, add them to the pan and fry them for 5 minutes. Add the rabbit, wood pigeon, venison or pheasant, and brown the meat, stirring from time to time.

If using dried ceps, drain them and retain the strained liquid. Squeeze the ceps dry and finely chop them.

Add the wine, bay leaves and the tomatoes to the meat mixture, and allow the liquids to evaporate slightly before you add the dried ceps (if using), and salt and pepper.

Cover and cook the mixture gently for 15 minutes. If using dried ceps, you may need to add a little of the water reserved from soaking them. Remove the bay leaves.

Cook the pasta for 5–7 minutes or until al dente and drain. Toss the pasta in the sauce and serve sprinkled with the Parmesan cheese.

Farfalle alla Genovese

FARFALLE GENOESE-STYLE

See pages 48–52 if you want to make your own farfalle, but if you feel a little too lazy or rushed the alternative is to buy some, although it's worth remembering that the bought variety will be without eggs. The sauce itself is easy to make and quick.

◆

SERVES 4

6 tablespoons olive oil
1 large onion, peeled and finely chopped
2 × 1 lb (450 g) cartons or bottles creamed or pulped tomatoes
4 basil leaves, shredded
Salt
Freshly ground black pepper
1 lb (450 g) fresh farfalle (see pages 48–9 and 52)
2 eggs, lightly beaten
2 oz (50 g) freshly grated Pecorino cheese

◆

METHOD

Heat the oil and fry the onion until soft. Add the tomatoes and cook for 10 minutes. Add the basil, salt and pepper.

Meanwhile, cook the pasta for 1–2 minutes or until al dente and drain. Just before serving gently reheat the sauce, whisking quickly whilst pouring in the beaten eggs. Do not allow the mixture to boil. When the sauce starts to thicken remove from the heat. Toss in the pasta and serve with the Pecorino cheese.

Maltagliati al sugo di melanzane

MALTAGLIATI WITH AUBERGINE SAUCE

Maltagliati means 'badly cut' and describes the irregular pieces of pasta which are cut out of the dough with a knife. This recipe is a dream, especially for vegetarians.

◆

SERVES 4

7 oz (200 g) aubergine

7 oz (200 g) carrots

6 tablespoons olive oil

1 onion, peeled and finely sliced

1 clove garlic, peeled and finely chopped

1 tablespoon chopped basil

2 teaspoons chopped fresh rosemary or 1 teaspoon dried rosemary

3^1/$_2$ fl oz (100 ml) red wine

3^1/$_2$ fl oz (100 ml) water

^{1}/$_2$ vegetable stock cube

Salt

Freshly ground black pepper

1 tablespoon finely chopped parsley

1 lb (450 g) fresh maltagliati (see pages 48–9 and 53), or 14 oz (400 g) dried
pappardelle, cut into irregular pieces

3 oz (75 g) freshly grated Pecorino cheese

◆

METHOD

Peel the aubergine, discard the skin and cut the flesh lengthwise into slices and then large matchsticks ¼ inch (5 mm) thick. Peel the carrots and cut into similar matchsticks.

Put the olive oil over a high heat, add the onion, aubergine and carrots, and fry until soft, stirring continuously. Add the garlic, basil and rosemary, and cook for 5 minutes on a lower heat. Add the wine, water and the stock cube. Cook for 1–2 minutes to reduce the liquids. Add salt and pepper to taste and the parsley.

Meanwhile, cook the pasta until it is al dente, allowing 4–5 minutes for the maltagliati or 5–6 minutes for the pappardelle. Toss the pasta in the sauce and serve sprinkled with the Pecorino cheese.

Brandelli ai carciofi

·

BRANDELLI WITH ARTICHOKES

Brandelli is my own shape of pasta. I created it some years ago when I wanted freshly made pasta in no particular shape at all! So I just tore it apart into fairly large pieces. Brandelli means 'in tatters', which seemed appropriate enough. Simply break fresh sheets of pasta with your hands so that every piece is at least 2 inches (5 cm) in size. Having gone into some detail about the pasta, let me quickly tell you that the artichokes have to be fresh.

·

SERVES 4

4 fresh artichoke hearts
4 tablespoons olive oil
1 onion, peeled and finely sliced
1 tablespoon capers, rinsed
2 large, ripe tomatoes or 1 × 14 oz (400 g) tin chopped tomatoes
Salt
Freshly ground black pepper
1 lb (450 g) fresh brandelli (see pages 48–9 and 53)
1 oz (25 g) butter, roughly chopped
2 tablespoons roughly chopped parsley

·

METHOD

Trim the artichokes, discard the tougher parts and cut them into very thin slices. Heat the oil and fry the artichoke slices with the onion over a low heat until the artichoke and the onion are soft. Add the capers and the tomatoes, salt and pepper, and cook for another 10 minutes.

Meanwhile, cook the pasta for 3–4 minutes or until al dente. Drain the pasta and toss in the sauce. Add the butter and serve sprinkled with the parsley. (No cheese is added.)

Brandelli agli asparagi

◆

BRANDELLI WITH ASPARAGUS SAUCE

This is another sauce suitable for my brandelli shapes (see Brandelli ai carciofi, page 79). Based on asparagus, it is delicious in late spring when the asparagus season is at its height.

◆

SERVES 4

1 lb (450 g) large asparagus spears
3 oz (75 g) butter
1 large onion, peeled and finely sliced
3 tablespoons milk
1 lb (450 g) fresh brandelli (see pages 48–9 and 53)
3 oz (75 g) finely grated Parmesan cheese
Salt
Freshly ground black pepper

◆

METHOD

Peel and trim the asparagus, then cook it in boiling water for 15 minutes or until tender. Remove the asparagus from the pan and cut about 2 inches (5 cm) off the top and set on one side to keep warm. Cut the lower part of the asparagus stems into ½ inch (1 cm) pieces.

Heat the butter in a pan, and gently fry the onion until just soft. Add the small asparagus stem pieces and the milk and cook for another 5–6 minutes. Mash the asparagus with a fork until the sauce is smooth.

Meanwhile, cook the pasta for 3–4 minutes or until al dente. Drain and mix with the sauce and add the Parmesan cheese. Toss well, add salt and pepper and serve with the asparagus tips as a garnish.

Orecchiette con broccoli

ORECCHIETTE WITH BROCCOLI

This home-made pasta is so good that it is well worth making extra and freezing some. Although fresh, these shapes take a little longer to cook than you might expect. You can buy ready-made, dried orecchiette from good delicatessens. They will need to be cooked for 15–18 minutes.

SERVES 4

1 lb (450 g) fresh or frozen broccoli

Salt

6 tablespoons olive oil

3 oz (75 g) speck or lean smoked bacon, rinded and
cut into small strips

2 cloves garlic, peeled and finely chopped

½ pint (300 ml) milk

1 lb (450 g) fresh orecchiette (see pages 48–9 and 53)

2 oz (50 g) freshly grated Parmesan cheese

Freshly ground black pepper

METHOD

Boil the broccoli in salted water until tender and drain. Chop the broccoli very finely. Heat the oil and fry the speck or bacon until brown. Add the garlic and cook for another minute. Add the broccoli and salt, and then stir in the milk. Cook the sauce, stirring until smooth.

Meanwhile, cook the pasta for 6 minutes or until al dente. Drain and add to the sauce. Toss well with the Parmesan cheese, add some black pepper and serve.

Pasta Fresca Ripiena

·

FRESH
FILLED PASTA

The techniques needed to produce fresh, stuffed or filled pasta are various, from using just your hands to using little gadgets like the raviola-trice, which is a flat, aluminium grid with cavities for producing ravioli. Whichever way you make it, the effort of preparing filled pasta yourself really pays off. You can make filled pasta a day ahead and store it in the refrigerator in a sealed container. I am a little more wary

about freezing filled pasta because you have to be sure that the filling will keep well, and that it cooks right through when you bring it out of the freezer. The alternative of buying fresh, filled pasta from a local supplier is only to be considered when you already trust their quality. Although it is very quick and easy to use the semi-fresh, vacuum-packed, filled pastas I wouldn't recommend them, because usually the taste of the filling is slightly artificial – and certainly nothing like as good as in the recipes shown here. Because it is usual for pasta fillings themselves to contain various ingredients, the sauces which accompany filled pasta are kept very simple. Sometimes we just use a little butter and cheese.

Ravioli di spinaci e ricotta

RAVIOLI WITH SPINACH

Di magro is how they describe this ravioli in Emilia, but it is called agnolotti in Piedmont. Both names refer to its meatless filling, usually based on ricotta cheese and a green leaf vegetable. The ravioli in this recipe are square (you can make round ravioli too, called tortelli), and different sizes are called ravioloni, ravioli or raviolini (respectively, from the largest to the smallest). Try them – they're really very easy to make.

SERVES 4

9 oz (250 g) fresh spinach or Swiss chard
Salt
5 oz (150 g) ricotta cheese
2 teaspoons freshly grated nutmeg
Freshly ground black pepper
2 egg yolks
3 oz (75 g) freshly grated Parmesan cheese
1 lb (450 g) fresh pasta dough (see pages 48–9)
3 oz (75 g) unsalted butter
4 sage leaves, finely chopped

METHOD

To make the filling: cook the spinach or chard in a little salted water, drain well, squeeze out the excess moisture and roughly chop. Mix the ricotta cheese with the spinach or chard. Stir in the nutmeg, salt, pepper, egg yolks and 1 oz (25 g) of the Parmesan cheese.

To make the ravioli: roll out the pasta dough on a lightly floured surface to two sheets of pasta about 1/8 inch (3 mm) thick and both approximately 14 1/2 × 9 1/2 inches (37 × 24 cm) in size.

Put heaped teaspoonfuls of the filling on one sheet of pasta, 2 inches (5 cm) apart. Cover with the other sheet of pasta. Press gently with your fingers all round the filling to seal the ravioli shapes, without air bubbles. Cut the pasta into squares with a pastry wheel, and lay the ravioli on a clean tea towel.

Cook the pasta for 4–5 minutes. Meanwhile, melt the butter. Drain the pasta and mix with the butter. Scatter with the sage and serve with the remaining Parmesan.

Ravioloni di pesce

·

RAVIOLONI WITH FISH

Here we use the largest ravioloni which are about 3 inches (7.5 cm) square. Don't make the delicious fish filling too smooth: it is better to keep a little texture to it. This recipe takes more effort than some, so you may wish to save it for special occasions.

◆

SERVES 4

5 oz (150 g) monkfish fillet
5 oz (150 g) fresh salmon fillet
3 oz (75 g) fresh, cooked, peeled prawns
2 tablespoons chopped dill, plus a few dill fronds to garnish
2 egg yolks
Salt
Freshly ground black pepper
1^1/$_2$ lb (750 g) fresh pasta dough (see pages 48–9)
2 oz (50 g) butter
1 sachet saffron powder or a pinch of saffron strands

◆

METHOD

To make the filling: poach the monkfish and salmon together in simmering water for 12–15 minutes until cooked. Roughly chop the cooked fish and prawns, removing any bones. Stir in the chopped dill, egg yolks, salt and pepper and mix well.

To make the ravioloni: roll out the pasta dough on a lightly floured surface to make two sheets of pasta about ^{1}/$_8$ inch (3 mm) thick and both approximately 20 × 10 inches (50 × 25 cm) in size (see Ravioli instructions, page 51).

Arrange 8 heaped teaspoonfuls of the fish filling on one sheet of pasta, 2^1/$_2$ inches (6 cm) apart. Cover with the other sheet of pasta. Press gently with your fingers all round the filling to seal the ravioloni shapes, without air bubbles. Cut the pasta into squares with a pastry wheel and lay the ravioloni on a clean tea towel. Cook the pasta for 5–6 minutes.

Meanwhile, melt the butter, adding the saffron powder. If using saffron strands, pound them to a powder with a pestle and mortar before adding. Drain the pasta.

Serve two large ravioloni on each plate with a little of the butter on top and garnish with the fronds of dill. (No need to use cheese.)

ANOLINI AL POMODORO (right)
See page 93
GNOCCHETTI SARDI CON ASPARAGI (left)
See page 117

Tortelloni di carne

TORTELLONI WITH MEAT

Here is another dish for special occasions, where you can prepare the tortelloni the day before and store them in the refrigerator. It requires a certain amount of skill to put tortelloni together, but I think that by now if you have made all the previous recipes, you are an expert so this task will be easier for you! This is the classic way to make tortelloni.

SERVES 6

4 oz (100 g) lean pork
4 oz (100 g) chicken or turkey breast
4 oz (100 g) beef marrow, extracted from
the bone (optional)
4 oz (100 g) butter
3 oz (75 g) Parma ham
4 oz (100 g) mortadella
3 tablespoons chopped parsley
8 oz (225 g) freshly grated Parmesan cheese
$^3/_4$ teaspoon freshly grated nutmeg
3 eggs, lightly beaten
Salt
Freshly ground black pepper
$1^1/_2$ lb (750 g) fresh pasta dough (see pages 48–9)
9 sage leaves

METHOD

To make the filling: roughly chop the pork, chicken or turkey, and the marrow (if using). Heat 1 oz (25 g) of the butter and fry the meats until brown. Put the meats in a food processor with the Parma ham, mortadella and parsley and blend to a smooth paste.

Fold 5 oz (150 g) of the Parmesan cheese into the paste. Stir in the nutmeg, eggs, salt and plenty of black pepper. Mix well, cover and leave the filling to stand for 1–2 hours.

To make the tortelloni: roll out the pasta dough on a lightly floured surface to $^1/_8$ inch (3 mm) thickness. Using a knife cut out squares 3 inches (7.5 cm) in size.

Place a teaspoonful of filling in the centre of each square, fold one corner over to make a triangle, and press the edges lightly together (see Cappellacci instructions, page 51). Gently bring the corners of the triangles together to make circular shapes. Lay the tortelloni on a clean tea towel.

Cook the pasta for 4–5 minutes. Meanwhile, melt the remaining butter, and add the sage leaves. Drain the pasta and mix with the butter and sage. Sprinkle with the remaining Parmesan cheese.

VARIATION

Tortellini alla panna

◆

TORTELLINI WITH CREAM

Tortellini are nothing else than a smaller version of tortelloni. Old women in the region of Emilia Romagna, towards the north of Italy, make tortellini which are very small indeed. I have never discovered how they can turn the tortellini, or cappelletti as they are known there, around their fingers.

◆

METHOD

Follow the method in Tortelloni di carne (opposite) for making the pasta shapes, but this time cut the squares 2 inches (5 cm) in size. Continue as before, bringing the corners of the triangles together to make filled circles of pasta.

Cook the pasta for 5–6 minutes and drain. Toss well in $^{1}/_{4}$ pint (150 ml) double cream instead of using butter and sage, and gently heat through. Serve simply with plenty of black pepper.

Raviolo aperto con pesce

OPEN RAVIOLO WITH FISH

This recipe is very popular in my restaurant and will certainly attract the attention of your guests! You can make the filling with vegetables, meat or fish. This is the fish version. I'm leaving it to your imagination to create the meat or vegetarian alternative.

If you wish to make it more colourful try using two different colours of pasta.

◆

SERVES 6

3 lb (1.5 kg) mussels (about 48)
1$\frac{1}{2}$ lb (750 g) fresh pasta dough (see pages 48–9)
6 oz (175 g) shelled scallops
6 oz (175 g) fresh salmon fillet
6 oz (175 g) monkfish or any other firm white fish fillet
4 oz (100 g) butter
1 clove garlic, peeled and very finely chopped
Salt
Freshly ground black pepper
1 tablespoon finely chopped parsley
1$\frac{1}{2}$ tablespoons finely chopped dill, plus dill fronds to garnish
2 tablespoons white wine
1 egg yolk, lightly beaten with $\frac{1}{4}$ teaspoon lemon juice (optional)
Olive oil

◆

METHOD

Scrub the mussels under cold running water, discarding any that are cracked or open. With a small sharp knife scrape away the beard. Wash the mussels in several changes of cold water until the water is left clean. Put the mussels in a large bowl, cover with cold water and leave to stand for 30 minutes. Drain and discard any with open shells, or that do not close when tapped against a hard surface.

Put the mussels in a large pan with just enough water to cover the bottom. Cover the pan and shake from time to time over a fairly high heat for about 5 minutes until all the shells have opened. Drain and take the mussel meat out of the shells. Discard any mussels that remain closed.

Roll out the pasta dough on a lightly floured surface to make three sheets of pasta each about 10 inches (25 cm) square, and ⅛ inch (3 mm) thick. Cut each sheet into 4 squares. Lay the 12 squares on clean tea towels.

Cut the scallops, salmon and monkfish into ¼ inch (5 mm) pieces.

Heat 2 oz (50 g) of the butter and fry the garlic for a few seconds. Add salt, pepper and the chopped fish, and continue to fry for a few minutes. Stir in the parsley, the chopped dill and the wine, and let the alcohol evaporate for 1 minute. If the filling mixture seems too thin, bind it by beating in the egg yolk and lemon juice.

Bring a pan of salted water to the boil, adding a tablespoon of oil. Put the pasta sheets into the water one at a time to prevent sticking. Cook the pasta for 4 minutes. Meanwhile, melt the remaining butter. Carefully remove the pasta and pat dry on clean tea towels.

While the pasta is still warm put one square on each of six warmed serving dishes. Divide the fish filling into six portions and place in the centre of each square. Using the remaining six pasta squares, cover the filling. Drizzle the melted butter on top and garnish each with a frond of dill.

Ravioli

Agnolotti con ricotta al tartufo

AGNOLOTTI WITH RICOTTA & TRUFFLE

In Piedmont, where the Western and Central Alps dominate, there is a tendency towards extremely refined and sophisticated food, crowned by the most expensive ingredient of all – the white Alba truffle. Agnolotti is the name the Piedmontese people commonly use for ravioli.

I include this rather unusual recipe because if at all possible I would like you to have the extraordinary experience of tasting the famous white truffle, or even the rather more mild, black one! As a last resort use 1 tablespoon truffle oil instead (from good Italian delicatessens) and reduce the quantity of butter to 1 oz (25 g).

♦

SERVES 4

11 oz (300 g) ricotta cheese
1 tablespoon finely chopped parsley
1 tablespoon finely chopped basil
1 tablespoon finely chopped mint
2 egg yolks
Pinch of freshly grated nutmeg
Salt
Freshly ground black pepper
2 oz (50 g) freshly grated Parmesan cheese
1 lb (450 g) fresh pasta dough (see pages 48–9)
2 oz (50 g) butter
1 small fresh white (or black) truffle, very finely sliced

♦

METHOD

To make the filling: mix the ricotta with the parsley, basil, mint, egg yolks, nutmeg, salt and pepper, and half the Parmesan cheese.

To make the agnolotti: roll out the pasta dough on a lightly floured surface to a thickness of about 1/8 inch (3 mm). Cut the pasta into two sheets of the same size. Put teaspoonfuls of the filling on one sheet 2 inches (5 cm) apart. Cover with the other sheet of pasta, press gently with your fingers all round the filling to seal the agnolotti shapes, without air bubbles. Cut the pasta into squares with a pastry wheel and lay them on a clean tea towel.

Cook the pasta for 4–5 minutes and drain.

Melt the butter and mix with the pasta. Serve sprinkled with the remaining Parmesan cheese and the truffle slices on top – divided very fairly between portions!

Anolini al pomodoro

ANOLINI WITH TOMATOES

Think of this as a sort of pasta exam – if you pass this you will be able to impress everyone! Anolini are the smallest filled pasta to be found, and it does take time to wind the shapes round your fingers, not least because everyone will eat so many of them. Having said that, it is impossible to manufacture anolini commercially, so you really will appreciate the effort of making your own. You could always invite your friends to help in the preparation, whilst you catch up on the gossip!

SERVES 6

1 quantity Tortelloni di carne (see page 88 and method below)
1 oz (25 g) butter
1 large onion, peeled and chopped
1 × 1 lb (450 g) carton or bottle creamed or pulped tomatoes
Few basil leaves
3 oz (75 g) freshly grated Parmesan cheese

METHOD

Follow the method in Tortelloni di carne (see page 88) for making the filling and pasta shapes, but this time cut the squares 1¾ inches (3 cm) in size. Continue as before, bringing the corners of the triangles together to make filled circles of pasta.

Next make a basic tomato sauce. Heat the butter and fry the onion until transparent. Add the tomatoes and basil. Cover and simmer gently for at least ½ an hour, stirring from time to time. If the mixture becomes too dry add a little chicken stock or water during the cooking time.

Cook the pasta for 3–4 minutes and drain. Serve with the tomato sauce and sprinkle with the Parmesan cheese.

CAPELLI D'ANGELO NERI CON CAPESANTE
See page 121
RAVIOLO APERTO CON PESCE (left)
See page 90

Uovo in raviolo al tartufo

EGG IN RAVIOLO WITH WHITE TRUFFLES

I got this idea while I was filming a food programme for the BBC in Imola near Bologna. The chef of the San Domenico, one of the best restaurants in Italy, prepared a dish I have never seen before and I was so impressed by it that I created a variation, as shown here. Unfortunately, when we did the photography, no white truffle was available, so we used black (see overleaf). But white would be best!

SERVES 4

FOR THE PASTA

7 oz (200 g) plain flour

2 egg yolks

Generous pinch of salt

FOR THE FILLING

1½ lb (750 g) fresh spinach

7 oz (200 g) ricotta or cottage cheese

Pinch of freshly grated nutmeg

2 oz (50 g) freshly grated Parmesan cheese

Salt

Freshly ground black pepper

4 egg yolks

2 tablespoons melted butter

1½ oz (40 g) white truffle, finely sliced, or 2 tablespoons finely
chopped fresh sage, or both

METHOD

Follow the instructions on pages 48–9 for making the pasta dough but using the quantities specified for this recipe.

To make the filling: cook the spinach in a little water. Drain when cool, squeeze out most of the remaining water, first of all between two strong plates and then with your hands, until fairly dry. Finely chop the spinach. Mix together the spinach, ricotta or cottage cheese, the nutmeg, half of the Parmesan cheese and salt and pepper to taste.

Lightly flour your work surface and a rolling pin. Gently roll the pasta dough out, rotating it in quarter turns. Using a little more flour as you need it, to prevent the pasta sticking, roll out the dough to two sheets of pasta each 12 inches (30 cm) square and ⅛ inch (3 mm) thick. Cut each sheet of pasta into four 6 inch (15 cm) squares.

Fill a piping bag fitted with a large nozzle with the spinach mixture, and pipe a fairly deep circle of the mixture on to each of 4 squares, leaving a space in the centre. Spoon one egg yolk, taking care not to break it, into each space. Brush the edges of the 4 squares with a little water, and gently cover with one of the plain pasta squares, pressing gently round the edges with your fingers to seal the ravioli shapes, without air bubbles. Trim the edges to a ½ inch (1 cm) border using a pastry wheel. (Alternatively cut round an upturned tea cup to make the ravioli shape.)

Gently immerse the pasta in a pan of boiling, salted water and cook for 1–2 minutes. Remove and serve on a warmed plate, with the melted butter, and the remaining Parmesan cheese and the thinly sliced truffle and/or sage sprinkled on top.

UOVO IN RAVIOLO: *Cut out two 6 inch (15 cm) squares of pasta. Place a circle of filling in the centre and put an egg yolk into it.*

2 *Place the second piece of pasta over the filling with the egg.*

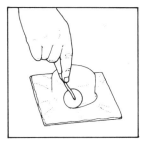

3 *Press out the air and cut around the raviolo about ½ inch (1 cm) from the filling.*

UOVO IN RAVIOLO AL TARTUFO
See page 96

Cannelloni

·

CANNELLONI

This really doesn't need any translation as it is well-known all over the world that cannelloni can be made in thousands of ways. Fillings are made from meat, fish or vegetables, or a mixture. In principle the filling is wrapped in a small sheet of cooked pasta, then baked with a tomato sauce. You can used dried cannelloni which are ready to be filled, but if you do buy these allow extra cooking time. As usual, the fresher the ingredients, the better, especially if you intend freezing the pasta.

Many people like to use a béchamel or white sauce to cover the cannelloni when baking it but I find this a little rich so I have not included it here. Use a sauce if you like to.

◆

SERVES 4

1 lb (450 g) fresh pasta dough (see pages 48–9)
Olive oil
1 oz (25 g) dried ceps or 7 oz (200 g) fresh cep mushrooms
2 oz (50 g) butter
1 small onion, peeled and very finely sliced
14 oz (400 g) lean minced beef
Salt
Freshly ground black pepper
Pinch of freshly grated nutmeg
1 egg yolk
2 tablespoons finely chopped parsley
1 Mozzarella cheese, cut into 8 segments
1 quantity Sugo di pomodoro (see page 44)
3 oz (75 g) freshly grated Parmesan cheese

◆

METHOD

Pre-heat the oven to 220°C/425°F/gas mark 7.

To make the cannelloni: roll out the pasta dough on a lightly floured surface to make two sheets of pasta each 10 inches (25 cm) square and ⅛ inch (3 mm) thick. Cut each sheet into 4 squares. Lay the 8 squares of pasta on a clean tea towel.

Cook the pasta for 4 minutes, adding the squares one by one to plenty of boiling water to which you have added 1 tablespoon oil, to prevent the pasta sticking. Carefully remove the pasta and pat dry on a clean tea towel.

If using dried ceps, soak them in warm water for 20 minutes. Drain and retain the strained liquid. Squeeze the ceps dry and finely chop them. If using fresh ceps finely chop them.

To make the filling: heat the butter and fry the onion until soft. Add the beef and the ceps and continue frying until the beef is browned. Add salt, pepper and nutmeg to taste and set aside to cool slightly.

Next, stir the egg yolk and the parsley into the filling mixture and mix well. Divide the filling between the eight pasta squares, spooning it down the middle of each piece of pasta.

Place a segment of Mozzarella on top of the filling and roll the pasta squares round the filling to make cannelloni tubes. Put 2 tablespoons Sugo di pomodoro in the bottom of a large ovenproof dish. Lay the cannelloni, side by side, over the sauce and cover with the remaining sauce. Sprinkle with the Parmesan cheese and bake in the pre-heated oven for 20 minutes. Serve immediately.

LASAGNE VEGETARIANE
See page 104

Lasagne vegetariane

◆

VEGETARIAN LASAGNE

Various versions of this famous dish exist, according to regional and personal preferences. I created this rather sumptuous version to satisfy the growing requests for imaginative pasta dishes without meat. As in the previous recipes in this section you need to allow plenty of time for the preparation. The consolation is the wonderful result which will fully justify your efforts. You can prepare this dish and assemble it up 24 hours in advance, keep it in the refrigerator, and then bake it in the oven when required.

◆

SERVES 6–8

1¼ lb (550 g) fresh pasta verde dough (see pages 48–9) or 1 lb (450 g)
dried green lasagne

Salt

Olive oil

3 lb (1.5 kg) fresh spinach

1 egg, lightly beaten (for the spinach balls)

2 tablespoons dried breadcrumbs

5 oz (150 g) freshly grated Parmesan cheese

Freshly grated nutmeg

Freshly ground black pepper

2 large aubergines, cut lengthwise into ¼ inch (5 mm) slices

2 eggs, lightly beaten (for coating the aubergines and courgettes)

4 oz (100 g) white flour

2 large courgettes, cut lengthwise into ¼ inch (5 mm) slices

11 oz (300 g) fresh oyster mushrooms or shiitake mushrooms, sliced

1 clove garlic, peeled and chopped

1 tablespoon chopped parsley

Double quantity Sugo di pomodoro (see page 44)

11 oz (300 g) Fontina or Taleggio cheese, cut into chunks

7 eggs, lightly beaten (for assembling the lasagne)

◆

METHOD

Pre-heat the oven to 190°C/375°F/gas mark 5.

To make the lasagne: roll out the pasta dough (if using fresh) on a lightly floured surface to make a single sheet ⅛ inch (3 mm) thick. Cut into rectangles about 4 × 8 inches (10 × 20 cm) in size.

Cook the fresh or dried pasta, adding the pieces one by one to boiling water to which you have added salt and 1 tablespoon oil, to prevent the pasta sticking. Allow 5 minutes cooking time for fresh pasta, 8–10 minutes for dried. Carefully remove the pasta and pat dry on clean tea towels.

To make the spinach balls: cook the spinach in a little water until tender, drain well and chop finely. Mix the spinach with 1 tablespoon beaten egg, the dried breadcrumbs and 1 oz (25 g) of the Parmesan cheese. Add nutmeg, salt and pepper to taste. Using your hands, shape the spinach mixture into walnut-sized balls.

Heat enough oil to deep fry the spinach balls, until lightly browned on all sides. Remove with a slotted spoon and set aside on paper towels.

To prepare the aubergines: put half of the 2 beaten eggs in a dish. Dip the aubergine slices into the flour and then into the beaten eggs. Heat enough oil to deep fry the aubergine, until golden. Remove with a slotted spoon and set aside on paper towels.

Prepare the courgettes in the same way as the aubergines, dipping them into flour and beaten egg, then deep frying them. Set aside on paper towels.

To prepare the mushrooms: heat 1 tablespoon oil in a separate frying pan, add the mushroom slices and fry briefly. Stir in the garlic and parsley, with salt and pepper to taste.

To assemble the lasagne: put 3–4 tablespoons Sugo di pomodoro on the bottom of a large baking dish. Cover with a layer of pasta. Next add a layer each of the mushrooms, the courgettes, aubergine, and spinach balls. Add some of the Fontina or Taleggio cheese. Now add 3–4 tablespoons tomato sauce, 3–4 tablespoons of the 7 beaten eggs, and a generous sprinkle of the remaining Parmesan cheese.

Starting with a layer of pasta, repeat the sequence of layers until the ingredients are all used, finishing with a layer of vegetables and cheeses.

Bake in the pre-heated oven for 20 minutes. Cut into portions and serve.

Pasta Secca all' Uovo

·

DRIED
EGG PASTA

When you really grow to love pasta you will understand why certain sauces go better with fresh pasta, certain sauces better with dried. The two different textures of pasta deserve different treatment. However, if you really want to try the sauces from the fresh pasta chapter with some of the dried pastas I won't be too horrified; although the result will not be quite as good.

Dried egg pasta, pasta secca all'uovo, is very brittle in its uncooked state, which is why it usually comes in reinforced

packages to protect it, and is often coiled round like a nest. Look for the words all'uovo on the packet, meaning with eggs. The better brands show how many eggs per kg of flour were used (usually a minimum of 6).

When cooking dried egg pasta you usually need about twice the cooking time you'd allow for the fresh equivalent. You have to really overcook dried egg pasta for it to go soft and soggy. Egg pasta is richer, with more protein, than plain pasta, and more filling. You will find it swells considerably during cooking – so you can be a little less generous with the portions.

Taglierini ai tre formaggi

TAGLIERINI WITH THREE CHEESES

Taglierini (also known as tagliolini) are ribbons just $1/8$ inch (3 mm) wide. The name of this recipe always reminds me of the pizza with four cheeses, which I don't particularly like. Anyway in this recipe these three cheeses complement each other nicely. Buon appetito!

♦

SERVES 4

$3/4$ oz (20 g) butter
4 oz (100 g) cooked unsmoked ham, cut into small cubes
2 oz (50 g) dolcelatte or Gorgonzola cheese, cut into small cubes
4 oz (100 g) mascarpone cheese
11 oz (300 g) dried egg taglierini
3 oz (75 g) freshly grated Parmesan cheese

♦

METHOD

Heat the butter and gently fry the ham, without letting it brown. Add the dolcelatte or Gorgonzola cheese and the mascarpone cheese and gently melt the cheeses over a low heat.

Cook the pasta for 4–5 minutes or until al dente, and drain. Mix with the cheese sauce. Sprinkle with the Parmesan cheese.

Taglierini ai tre funghi

THREE-MUSHROOM TAGLIERINI

After the three cheeses, the three mushrooms, two of which are very much a springtime affair. Fresh chanterelles and morels are sold in good delicatessens during the spring and early summer. Fresh ceps are available from August until late October. If you can't find the fresh variety I suggest you use 1 oz (25 g) each of any two of the mushrooms in their dried form and add 4 oz (100 g) cultivated oyster mushrooms (or even button mushrooms) for freshness. If you do this you will need to soak the dried mushrooms in the usual way (see page 32).

♦

SERVES 4

3 oz (75 g) butter
1 small onion, peeled and finely chopped
2 oz (50 g) Parma ham, finely chopped
4 oz (100 g) fresh chanterelles, sliced
4 oz (100 g) fresh morels, sliced
4 oz (100 g) fresh cep mushrooms, sliced
11 oz (300 g) dried egg taglierini
3 tablespoons double cream (optional)
Salt
Freshly ground black pepper
3 oz (75 g) freshly grated Parmesan cheese

♦

METHOD

Heat the butter and fry the onion until golden. Add the Parma ham, fry for a few minutes, then add the fresh mushrooms. Cook for 15 minutes.

Cook the pasta for 5 minutes or until al dente, and drain. Toss with the mushrooms and cream (if using), add salt and pepper to taste, and sprinkle with the Parmesan cheese.

TAGLIERINI AI TRE FUNGHI
See page 109

Fettuccine al salmone

FETTUCCINE WITH SMOKED SALMON

This is one of the recipes I created using a typically British ingredient – smoked salmon. The sauce is very easy to prepare and is well suited to any of the flat egg pastas.

◆

SERVES 4

13 oz (375 g) dried egg fettuccine
3 oz (75 g) butter, cut into small cubes
9 oz (250 g) smoked salmon, cut into strips
2 tablespoons finely chopped dill
Salt
Freshly ground black pepper

◆

METHOD

Cook the pasta for 10–12 minutes or until al dente, and drain. Whilst very hot add the butter, the salmon and the dill. Taste for salt and add generous amounts of black pepper.

Fettuccine verdi d'estate

SUMMERTIME GREEN FETTUCCINE

This recipe gets its name because of the importance of having those wonderfully ripe, Mediterranean tomatoes, which are at their best in summer. I also think the uncooked tomatoes in the sauce are lovely on a sultry summer's day.

◆

SERVES 4

1 lb (450 g) large ripe Mediterranean tomatoes
4 tablespoons virgin olive oil
1 clove garlic, peeled and crushed
10 basil leaves, finely chopped
Pinch of freshly chopped oregano or marjoram
Salt
2 oz (50 g) freshly grated Pecorino cheese
11 oz (300 g) Mozzarella cheese, chopped into small cubes
13 oz (375 g) dried green egg fettuccine or tagliatelle

◆

METHOD

Plunge the tomatoes in boiling water for 1 minute. Drain them, and remove the skins. Roughly chop the flesh, discarding the seeds.

In a large ceramic bowl mix the tomatoes, oil and garlic, basil, oregano or marjoram, salt, Pecorino and Mozzarella cheeses and leave to marinate for 1 hour.

Cook the pasta for 10–12 minutes or until al dente. Drain, mix with the tomato mixture and serve.

LINGUE DI PASSERO CON SALSA CRUDA (right)
See page 130
SPAGHETTINI AI FRUTTI DI MARE (left)
See page 125

Pappardelle al sugo di quaglie

PAPPARDELLE WITH QUAIL SAUCE

I tried to discover where pappardelle comes from without success. It is the widest pasta, and extremely satisfying. In this dish the combination of quail and morels is wonderful. If you don't feel altogether confident about boning the quail yourself ask if your butcher will do it for you.

◆

SERVES 4

1 oz (25 g) dried morels
2 oz (50 g) butter
1 celery stick, very finely sliced
Breasts and livers of 4 quails, finely sliced
5 fl oz (150 ml) dry red wine
Salt
Freshly ground black pepper
4 tablespoons double cream (optional)
13 oz (375 g) dried egg pappardelle
3 oz (75 g) freshly grated Parmesan cheese

◆

METHOD

Soak the morels in warm water for 20 minutes or until soft. Drain and squeeze them dry, retaining the strained soaking liquid. Slice the larger mushrooms and leave the smaller ones whole.

Heat the butter and gently fry the celery. When softened add the sliced quail and livers, and fry for a few minutes. Add the morels and stir in the wine. Let the wine evaporate for 2–3 minutes. Stir in 2–3 tablespoons of the reserved soaking liquid and cook for another few minutes. Add salt and pepper to taste. If you prefer a richer sauce, stir in the cream.

Cook the pasta for about 6 minutes or until al dente, and drain. Toss with the sauce, and mix well, adding the Parmesan cheese.

Capelli d'angelo al granchio

ANGEL'S HAIR WITH CRAB

This very fine type of pasta is usually sold in cellophane packets. It is extremely fragile and that is why it is only made in nests. When you buy it you should check that the strands are intact and that you're not taking home a lot of broken pieces. For this recipe you also need very fresh crab meat.

♦

SERVES 4

2 oz (50 g) butter
^{1}/$_2$ clove garlic, peeled and finely chopped
12 oz (350 g) freshly cooked white crab meat
1 × 1 lb (450 g) carton or bottle creamed or pulped tomatoes
Salt
Freshly ground black pepper
13 oz (375 g) dried egg capelli d'angelo
1 tablespoon finely chopped basil

♦

METHOD

Heat the butter and add the garlic, then the crab meat, stirring for 1 minute. Add the tomatoes. Mix well and cook for another minute. Add salt and plenty of pepper.

Meanwhile, cook the pasta for 3–4 minutes or until al dente, and drain. Mix well with the sauce and serve sprinkled with the basil.

Pasta Secca

·

DRIED
PLAIN PASTA

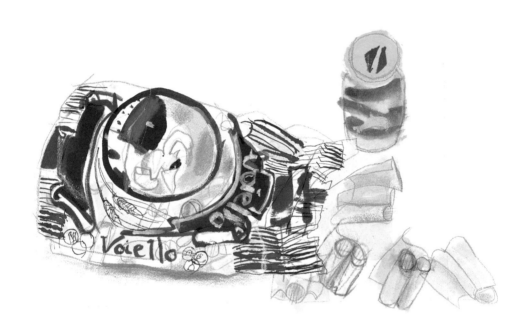

In Italian the words pasta secca describe the form which is made from durum wheat semolina and water, with no addition of eggs or other ingredients. It is by far the most widely used pasta in Italy, because it is more versatile and more economical than other pastas. As the dough is easier to work with than an egg pasta it can produce an enormous variety of shapes, as you will begin to see when you try different stockists. In some places in Italy it is still hand made and air dried, but generally it is now manufactured by modern machinery.

If you see the term pasta asciutta on a menu just remember that although translated as dried pasta, it has, in fact, nothing to do with the desiccation process, but refers to the way the pasta is served – it will arrive with just enough sauce to coat the shapes.

Gnocchetti sardi con asparagi

SARDINIAN GNOCCHETTI WITH ASPARAGUS

Of all the regional, hand-made pasta, Sardinian gnocchetti is probably the one that is reproduced most successfully by machine. Gnocchetti are usually combined with sauces based on tomatoes, but here I have used asparagus which softens to make a deliciously smooth sauce. Alternatively you could use my broccoli sauce in Orecchiette con broccoli (see page 81).

♦

SERVES 4

1 lb (450 g) fresh asparagus
$3^{1}/_{2}$ pints (2 litres) chicken stock (see page 36)
3 oz (75 g) unsalted butter
1 small onion, peeled and very finely chopped
Salt
Freshly ground black pepper
11 oz (300 g) dried gnocchetti sardi
3 oz (75 g) freshly grated Parmesan cheese

♦

METHOD

Scrape the asparagus, saving the peel. Cut off the top 2 inches (5 cm) and set aside. Bring the stock to the boil and gently simmer the asparagus, together with the peel for about 15 minutes or until soft. Add the asparagus tips for the last 10 minutes of cooking.

Lift the asparagus out of the stock with a slotted spoon and discard the peel. Retain the stock. Set the tips on one side for the garnish and keep warm. Cut the stems into $^{1}/_{2}$ inch (1 cm) lengths.

Heat the butter and fry the onion until golden. Add the chopped asparagus stems, and 2–3 tablespoons of the stock, salt and pepper, and cook for another few minutes. With the back of a fork mash the asparagus until a smooth pulp.

Meanwhile, cook the pasta in the retained stock for 10–12 minutes or until al dente, and drain. Reheat the sauce and toss well with the pasta and the Parmesan cheese. Serve garnished with the asparagus tips.

Capelli d'angelo neri con capesante

◆

BLACK ANGEL'S HAIR WITH SCALLOPS

I chose the black capelli d'angelo for this. Made with the addition of cuttlefish ink to give it its colour, and obtainable from the best Italian food shops, it combines with the very tender scallops to produce a wonderful marriage of taste, colour and texture. It is also an extremely quick recipe, taking just minutes to prepare.

◆

SERVES 4

14 oz (400 g), or 8 large, or 16 small, fresh scallops, cleaned
6 tablespoons virgin olive oil
1 clove garlic, peeled and finely chopped
1 small chilli pepper, finely chopped
$^{1}/_{4}$ pint (150 ml) dry white wine
2 tablespoons finely chopped parsley
Salt
13 oz (375 g) dried black capelli d'angelo

◆

METHOD

If using large scallops, detach the coral and cut the white meat into 4 slices (if using small scallops, leave them whole). Heat the oil and gently fry the garlic, chilli and white meat, with the corals, for 1 minute. Add the wine, parsley, and salt to taste.

Cook the pasta for 3–4 minutes, or until al dente, and drain. Add to the scallop mixture, mix well and serve.

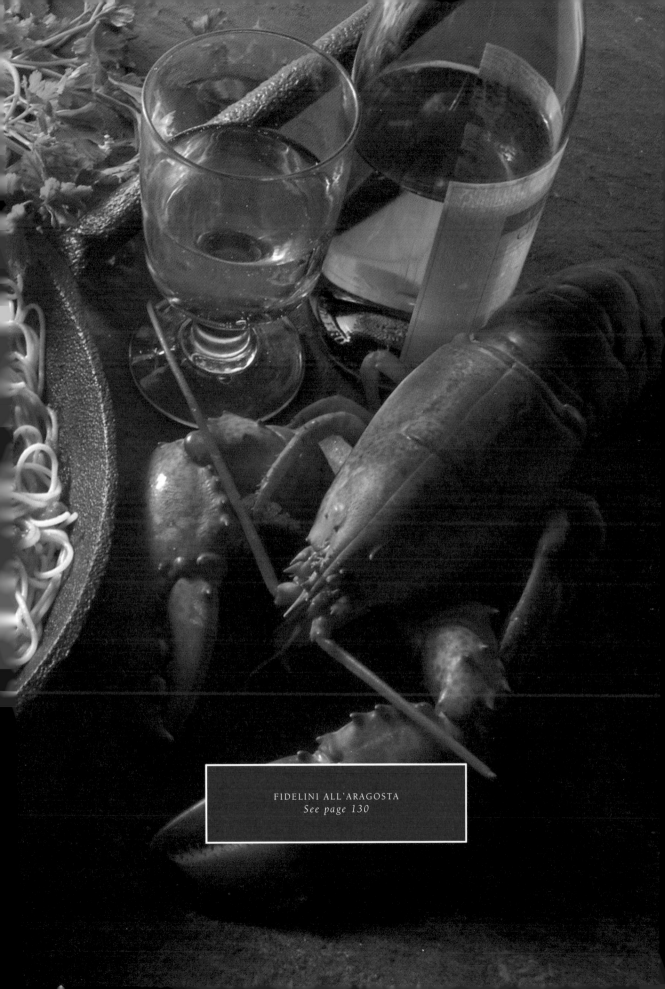

FIDELINI ALL'ARAGOSTA
See page 130

Spaghettini al pomodoro e basilico

SPAGHETTINI WITH TOMATO AND BASIL

This is one of the simplest sauces. If you use garlic instead of onion, and olive oil instead of butter, you obtain a Neapolitan sauce that is equally good. If you manage to find the best ripe tomatoes you can leave out the cheese because the taste will be rich and fine without it.

♦

SERVES 4

2 oz (50 g) butter
1 small onion, peeled and finely chopped, or 4 spring onions,
trimmed and finely chopped
3 large, ripe tomatoes, peeled, de-seeded and roughly chopped
8 basil leaves, shredded
Salt
14 oz (400 g) dried spaghettini
2 oz (50 g) freshly grated Parmesan cheese

♦

METHOD

Heat the butter and gently fry the onion or spring onions until beginning to brown. Add the tomatoes and fry for another 3–4 minutes. Add the basil, and salt to taste.

Meanwhile, cook the pasta for 5–7 minutes or until al dente. Mix with the sauce and serve sprinkled with the Parmesan cheese.

Spaghettini ai frutti di mare

SPAGHETTINI WITH SEAFOOD SAUCE

Almost everywhere, and especially in seaside restaurants in Italy, you can find this dish, which is made with any kind of local fresh, small mollusc or fish. You can use a small octopus, squid, mussels, clams, oysters, small prawns or scallops. If you are using clams or mussels make sure you clean them thoroughly. Follow the preparation guidelines described on pages 90 and 128. In some areas of Italy they add tomatoes but I prefer it without.

SERVES 4

6 tablespoons olive oil
1 clove garlic, peeled and finely chopped
1 chilli pepper, finely chopped (optional)
12 oz (350 g) mixed seafood (as suggested above), cleaned
2 tablespoons dry white wine
Salt
Freshly ground black pepper
13 oz (375 g) dried spaghettini
1 tablespoon finely chopped parsley

METHOD

Heat the oil and gently fry the garlic, and chilli, if using, until the garlic is slightly golden. Add the seafood, increase the heat and fry for 8–10 minutes, stirring continuously. Make sure that the clams and mussels are open at the end of the cooking time. If they are not, discard them. Pour in the wine and let it evaporate for 1 minute. Keep the mixture warm over a low heat and add salt and pepper to taste.

Meanwhile, cook the pasta for 5–7 minutes or until al dente, and drain. Mix with the sauce. Serve sprinkled with the parsley.

MARILLE AL SUGO CON PISELLI
See page 143

Vermicelli alle vongole

VERMICELLI WITH CLAM SAUCE

In Naples spaghetti are called vermicelli, which really means little worms!

The clams in this recipe should be the small, grey ones. Alternatively, try the Venus clam which is completely white, and very delicious. It is possible to use the tinned variety but remember most of its flavour disappears in the processing.

♦

SERVES 4

1 lb (450 g) fresh clams in their shells
6 tablespoons olive oil
1 clove garlic, peeled and chopped
1 small chilli pepper, finely chopped
1 × 14 oz (400 g) tin chopped tomatoes
Salt
Freshly ground black pepper
13 oz (375 g) dried vermicelli
1 tablespoon finely chopped parsley

♦

METHOD

Thoroughly wash the clams. Discard any broken ones and those that appear empty. Put the clams in a large pan with a lid and place over a low heat. Shake them in the pan from time to time until all the clam shells are open. There will be some 'milky' water at the bottom of the pan which should be reserved. Remove the clams and discard most of the shells, keeping some for a garnish.

Heat the oil in a separate pan and fry the garlic and the chilli without letting them brown. Add the tomatoes and cook for another 6–7 minutes. If the sauce needs more liquid add a little of the reserved cooking liquid. Add the clams and cook for another 1–2 minutes. Taste for salt, remembering that the clam water is already salty. Add pepper.

Meanwhile, cook the pasta for 7–8 minutes or until al dente, and drain. Mix with the sauce and serve sprinkled with the chopped parsley.

Lingue di passero all' acciuga

SPARROW TONGUES WITH ANCHOVIES

Don't worry, the term sparrow tongues is only the translation of the name of a type of pasta and nothing to do with a banquet of a Roman Emperor! This type of flat spaghetti is particularly suitable for a very simple sauce as given here.

◆

SERVES 4

10 anchovy fillets (salted or in oil)
3 oz (75 g) butter
1 clove garlic, peeled and very finely chopped
1 small chilli pepper, very finely chopped
12 oz (350 g) dried lingue di passero
1 tablespoon very finely chopped parsley

◆

METHOD

If using salted anchovies soak them in water for $^{1}/_{2}$ hour. Dry the anchovies on paper towels and remove any large bones.

Heat the butter, add the garlic and the chilli, and fry very gently until the garlic starts to brown. Take the pan off the heat and add the anchovy fillets. Stir until smooth.

Meanwhile, cook the pasta for 7–8 minutes or until al dente. Drain, adding 1–2 tablespoons of the pasta water to the anchovies, if necessary, to make a sauce. Toss the pasta with the sauce, and add the parsley.

Lingue di passero con salsa cruda

SPARROW TONGUES WITH EGG SAUCE

While I was putting together the ideas for these recipes I tried this combination which requires very little time and is especially delicious on those summer days when you don't want to be inside cooking. Various ingredients may be added like a little chopped chilli or cream and spinach but I prefer it like this.

SERVES 4

13 oz (375 g) dried lingue di passero or bavettine
2 tablespoons finely chopped parsley
2 tablespoons finely chopped basil
4 egg yolks
3 oz (75 g) freshly grated Parmesan cheese
8 tablespoons virgin olive oil
Salt
Freshly ground black pepper
Freshly grated nutmeg

METHOD

Cook the pasta for 7–8 minutes or until al dente. Meanwhile, in a bowl mix together the chopped parsley and basil with the egg yolks. Add the Parmesan cheese and the oil and stir well, adding salt, pepper and nutmeg to taste.

Drain the pasta, then mix with the sauce which, in contact with the heat of the pasta, will become deliciously smooth.

Fidelini all'aragosta

PASTA WITH LOBSTER

This rather posh-sounding recipe is a very common dish in parts of Italy where lobsters are caught. I think that fishermen are probably the only people to eat this cheaply because by the time lobsters arrive in the shops they are very expensive. However, you only need one 1½–2 lb (750 g–1 kg) lobster to make four servings of this wonderful, simple recipe. Fidelini are also known as spaghettini; or lingue di passero will do for this recipe. If you can't get lobster try using giant prawns.

♦

SERVES 4

1 × 1½–2 lb (750 g–1 kg) fresh lobster (or giant prawns,
shelled and cut into small pieces)
6 tablespoons olive oil
1 clove garlic, peeled and finely chopped
1½ lb (750 g) very ripe tomatoes, skinned, de-seeded and
chopped, or 2 × 14 oz (400 g) tins chopped tomatoes
2 tablespoons chopped flat-leaf parsley
2 tablespoons dry white wine
Salt
Freshly ground black pepper
14 oz (400 g) dried fidelini or lingue di passero

♦

METHOD

If using fresh lobster bring a large pan of water to the boil. Put the lobster in it and cover with a lid. Simmer over a low heat for 20 minutes. Take out the lobster and leave to cool.

Place the lobster on a board and using a sharp knife cut along the entire length of its back. Open out the two halves and remove the two gills (towards the head), the dark vein running down the tail, and the small stomach sac in the head. Do not discard the green, creamy liver in the head, as this is delicious. If it's a female lobster you should also retain the coral. Using a small skewer extract the tail meat. Crack open the large claws and remove the meat, discarding the thin membrane. Cut any larger pieces of meat into smaller pieces.

Heat the oil and gently fry the garlic. Add the tomatoes and the parsley and cook for another 10 minutes. Add the lobster (with any juices) to the sauce with the wine, and add salt and pepper to taste. If using prawns as an alternative to lobster, add them to the sauce at this point. Cook for 1–2 minutes to let the alcohol evaporate and heat the fish.

Meanwhile, cook the pasta for 7–8 minutes or until al dente, and drain. Toss with some of the sauce, and serve with the remaining sauce on top.

Trenette al pesto

TRENETTE WITH BASIL SAUCE

Trenette is the name the Genoese give linguine, where this world-famous pesto sauce comes from. Trenette (or linguine) have the same shape as the lingue di passero (sparrow tongues), but are slightly larger.

There are a few variations to this sauce, the basis of which should always be the very small-leafed variety of basil which is the one that grows on the Italian Riviera. The only thing that is indispensable in making a good pesto is a pestle and mortar. You can always produce a little more pesto than is needed this time, and keep it in an airtight container in the refrigerator for up to a week.

To eat the pesto as they do in Genoa you should serve some boiled potatoes and French beans with the pasta.

♦

SERVES 4

2 cloves garlic, peeled and roughly chopped
1½ oz (40 g) basil leaves
1 oz (25 g) pine kernels
½ teaspoon coarse sea salt
3 oz (75 g) freshly grated Parmesan or mature Pecorino cheese
6 tablespoons olive oil
13 oz (375 g) dried trenette

♦

METHOD

Put the garlic, basil and the pine kernels in a mortar. Add the salt. With the pestle, and trying to grind rather than pound the ingredients, use the coarseness of the salt to break down the ingredients. Gradually add the Parmesan or Pecorino cheese and continue to work the ingredients into a pulp.

Now, very slowly, add a stream of oil and, using the pestle, incorporate just enough oil to obtain a smooth green sauce.

Cook the pasta for 8–10 minutes or until al dente, and drain. Toss with the pesto and serve immediately.

Linguine al tonno

LINGUINE WITH TUNA FISH SAUCE

The flat, slightly rounded shape of this pasta particularly suits sauces based on fish. This recipe just goes to show how useful it is to keep a tin of tuna in the cupboard.

SERVES 4

4 tablepoons virgin olive oil
3 tablespoons finely chopped parsley
2 cloves garlic, peeled and finely chopped
1 small chilli pepper, finely chopped
$^1/_2$ inch (1 cm) fresh ginger root, peeled and thinly sliced
1 × 1 lb (450 g) carton or bottle creamed or pulped tomatoes
1 × 14 oz (400 g) tin tuna fish in oil, drained
and roughly chopped
Salt
13 oz (375 g) dried linguine
Freshly ground black pepper

METHOD

Heat the oil and gently fry 2 tablespoons of the parsley, the garlic, chilli and the ginger for a few minutes until slightly soft. Add the tomatoes and continue to cook for another few minutes. Stir in the tuna and a little salt.

Meanwhile, cook the pasta for 8–10 minutes or until al dente, and drain. Toss with the sauce and serve sprinkled with the remaining parsley and freshly ground pepper to taste.

PENNE RIGATE CON SALSICCIA
See page 144

Bucatini alla carbonara

BUCATINI WITH BACON, CHEESE AND EGGS

I don't believe this sauce needs any introduction. It is well-known in Britain although it is not always made as it should be! The eggs must not be cooked and it is this that gives the character to the sauce. In some places double cream is added too, but I think it then becomes too rich, although I leave this up to you.

Bucatini are also known as perciatelli, and are like spaghetti, but with a hollow centre. In the Lazio region, surrounding Rome, bucatini are used more often than spaghetti with this sauce. Pancetta, or air-cured bacon, helps produce the authentic flavour but you can substitute green or smoked bacon for it, although the result is a little different.

♦

SERVES 4

14 oz (400 g) dried bucatini
2 oz (50 g) butter or 6 tablespoons olive oil
4 oz (100 g) pancetta or bacon, rinded and cut into small strips
4 egg yolks
1 tablespoon milk
1¹/₂ oz (40 g) freshly grated mature Pecorino cheese
Freshly ground black pepper

♦

METHOD

Cook the pasta for 7–8 minutes or until al dente, and drain.

Meanwhile, heat the butter or oil and fry the pancetta or bacon until lightly browned, and set aside. Lightly beat the egg yolks and the milk in a bowl and add the Pecorino cheese. Pour the egg mixture into the bacon and add the pasta. Toss the hot pasta to coat it with the uncooked egg, which will set slightly on the pasta. Add plenty of black pepper.

Bucatini in salsa

◆

VENETIAN-STYLE BUCATINI

This recipe is a speciality of Venice because it is there that they make bigoli – a special type of pasta, much larger than the biggest spaghetti and without the hole. I like the pasta sauce so much that I decided to cheat a little and use bucatini instead which is easier to buy and produces very good results.

◆

SERVES 4

6 anchovy fillets (salted or in oil)
6 tablespoons olive oil
2 onions, peeled and finely sliced
13 oz (375 g) dried bucatini
Freshly ground black pepper

◆

METHOD

If using salted anchovies soak them in water for $^1/_2$ hour. Dry the anchovies on paper towels and remove any large bones.

Heat the oil, add the onions and 3 tablespoons water. Cover and cook very gently for 15–20 minutes, stirring occasionally, until the onions have softened considerably. Add the anchovies and stir well so they soften to make a sauce.

Meanwhile, cook the pasta for 7–8 minutes or until al dente, and drain. Toss with the sauce. Sprinkle with plenty of black pepper.

ORECCHIONI PICCANTI
See page 156

Maccheroncini con le sarde

MACARONI WITH SARDINES

Don't cook this recipe unless you find very fresh sardines. I once ordered this typical Sicilian speciality in an Italian restaurant much praised by a food critic as the best Italian restaurant of the year. I had to send the dish back because the taste and smell of cod liver oil, which is typical of old sardines, were repulsive. To make the dish genuine you should use wild fennel, but cultivated fresh fennel also gives excellent results. In this recipe one can see the Arabic influence which is often found in Sicilian cooking.

◆

SERVES 4

6 anchovy fillets (salted or in oil)
14 oz (400 g) fresh sardines
1 large fennel bulb
Salt
1 sachet saffron powder or a pinch of saffron strands
6 tablespoons olive oil
1 onion, peeled and finely chopped
1½ oz (40 g) raisins
1 oz (25 g) pine kernels
Freshly ground black pepper
13 oz (375 g) dried maccheroncini or bucatini

◆

METHOD

If using salted anchovies soak them in water for ½ hour. Dry the anchovies on paper towels and remove any large bones. Remove the sardine heads and tails, and slit the sardines open along the underside. Clean them thoroughly, removing the backbones.

Trim the fennel and cut into quarters and cook both the bulb and the leaves in slightly salted water for about 15 minutes or until tender. Remove the fennel and retain the cooking water. Once the fennel has cooled slightly roughly chop it. If using saffron strands put them in 2 tablespoons boiling water and leave until the water is coloured.

Heat the oil and fry the onion until golden. Add the anchovies and let them soften. Add the sardines and cook for another few minutes. Stir in the fennel, raisins, pine kernels and saffron powder, or strained liquid from soaking the strands. Add salt and pepper to taste, and cook briefly to make a smooth sauce.

Meanwhile, cook the pasta for 7–8 minutes or until al dente, and drain. Toss in the sauce.

Bucatini all'amatriciana

AMATRICE-STYLE BUCATINI

This Abruzzese recipe is typical of Amatrice, the farming town it comes from. It is also eaten a lot in Rome as Amatrice is on the border of Lazio. It is a classic in the Italian pasta repertoire.

SERVES 4

3 tablespoons olive oil
5 oz (150 g) pancetta or bacon, rinded and cut into strips
1 small onion, peeled and finely chopped
1 small chilli pepper, finely chopped
1 × 1 lb (450 g) carton or bottle creamed or pulped tomatoes
13 oz (375 g) dried bucatini
2 oz (50 g) freshly grated Pecorino cheese

METHOD

Heat the oil and fry the pancetta or bacon, the onion and the chilli for 3–4 minutes until slightly brown. Add the tomatoes, cover and cook gently for 10–15 minutes.

Meanwhile, cook the pasta for 7–8 minutes or until al dente, and drain. Toss in the sauce, and serve sprinkled with the Pecorino cheese.

Maccheroncini alla napoletana

NEAPOLITAN-STYLE MACARONI

Maccheroncini, or maccheroni, was invented in the region surrounding Naples. Neapolitan food is mainly known for the use of tomatoes and very little meat. Simple ingredients are, in fact, transformed into many different dishes, but a Neapolitan sauce needs little introduction, for it has become such a cookery classic.

SERVES 4

8 tablespoons olive oil
2 cloves garlic, peeled and finely chopped
1 small chilli pepper, finely chopped
2 × 1 lb (450 g) cartons or bottles creamed or pulped tomatoes
1 teaspoon concentrated tomato purée
3 tablespoons roughly chopped parsley.
Salt
13 oz (375 g) dried maccheroncini or bucatini
Freshly ground black pepper

METHOD

Heat the oil and fry the garlic and chilli for 2–3 minutes. Add the tomatoes and tomato purée, cover and cook gently for 10–15 minutes. Add the parsley, and salt to taste.

Meanwhile, cook the pasta for 7–8 minutes or until al dente, and drain. Toss the pasta with the sauce and sprinkle with freshly ground black pepper.

Marille al sugo con piselli

MARILLE WITH PEAS

The marille used for this recipe (and in the photograph on page 127) was the original 'designer pasta'. It was designed by Giugiaro, the famous Italian car designer, on behalf of one of the leading pasta manufacturers. But engaging Giugiaro was not just a publicity gag: marille's ribbed tubular shape held a large amount of sauce, the ultimate aim of the best pasta. So it is very sad that the production of marille has been discontinued. As an alternative, I suggest you use large gomiti.

◆

SERVES 4

2 oz (50 g) butter

5 oz (150 g) smoked bacon, rinded and cut into strips

1 × 1 lb (450 g) carton or bottle creamed or pulped tomatoes,
or 4 large ripe tomatoes, skinned and de-seeded

7 oz (200 g) frozen petits pois or small fresh peas

13 oz (375 g) marille or gomiti

8 basil leaves, shredded

5 oz (150 g) mascarpone cheese

Salt

Freshly ground black pepper

3 oz (75 g) freshly grated Parmesan cheese

◆

METHOD

Heat the butter and fry the bacon until crisp. Add the tomatoes and the petits pois or fresh peas, and cook for 5 minutes (or cover and cook for 15 minutes if using fresh peas).

Meanwhile, cook the pasta for 10–12 minutes or until al dente. Add the basil leaves and mascarpone cheese to the sauce and stir until just warmed through and the cheese has melted. Add salt and pepper to taste.

Drain the pasta and add to the sauce. Mix well with the Parmesan cheese.

Penne rigate con salsiccia

PENNE RIGATE WITH SAUSAGE

The ribbed penne rigate are very popular in Italy, and abroad too.

Usually an Italian trattoria offers them all'arrabbiata – with chilli (see Penne all'arrabbiata opposite); or with a tuna fish sauce. (They are also used in timbales.) This version is based on the best-quality pork sausage meat you can find (100% pork if possible) and it is very delicious.

♦

SERVES 4

3 oz (75 g) butter

1 small onion, peeled and chopped

1 clove garlic, peeled and finely chopped

11 oz (300 g) pork sausage meat or sausages (luganega type)

1 sprig rosemary, finely chopped

$^{1}/_{4}$ pint (150 ml) dry white wine

Pinch of freshly grated nutmeg

Pinch of ground cloves

Salt

Freshly ground black pepper

13 oz (375 g) dried penne rigate

3 oz (75 g) freshly grated Parmesan cheese

♦

METHOD

Heat the butter and gently fry the onion and the garlic. Break up the sausage meat with a fork (if using sausages, remove the skin before breaking up the meat). Add to the pan and gently fry until well browned. Add the rosemary, and the wine, and cook slowly for 10 minutes. Add the nutmeg, cloves, and salt and pepper.

Meanwhile, cook the pasta for 7–8 minutes or until al dente, and drain. Mix with the sausage mixture and the Parmesan cheese.

Penne all'arrabbiata

PENNE WITH CHILLI SAUCE

Arrabbiata means furious or angry. The ingredient that makes the pasta angry is the chilli and if you want the pasta to be very hot you just need to say to waiters 'molto arrabbiate' ('very angry') – and you will be served something which makes Indian food seem mild by comparison! Penne lisce are penne rigate without the ridges.

SERVES 4

6 tablespoons olive oil
2 cloves garlic, peeled and finely chopped
2 chilli peppers, finely chopped
1 × 14 oz (400 g) tin chopped tomatoes or 1 × 1 lb (450 g)
carton or bottle creamed or pulped tomatoes
Salt
13 oz (375 g) dried penne rigate or penne lisce
2 tablespoons finely chopped parsley
3 oz (75 g) freshly grated Parmesan or Pecorino cheese

METHOD

Heat the oil and briefly fry the garlic and the chilli. Add the tomatoes and cook for 15 minutes. Add salt to taste. Cook the pasta for 5–6 minutes or until al dente, and drain. Add the pasta and the parsley to the sauce and mix together with the Parmesan or Pecorino cheese.

PIZZOCCHERI VEGETARIANI
See page 157

Tortiglioni con funghi e formaggio

TORTIGLIONI WITH MUSHROOMS & CHEESE

Tortiglioni is another of the larger pastas that looks like a twisted, hollow macaroni. Sometimes tortiglioni goes by other names such as ricciolo, fusilli or eliceh. They are usually good with tomato-based sauces, but I would like you to try an exception. This sauce looks a little untidy but tastes delicious.

◆

SERVES 4

³/₄ oz (20 g) dried ceps
6 tablespoons olive oil
7 oz (200 g) button mushrooms, finely sliced
7 oz (200 g) ricotta cheese
4 oz (100 g) coarsely grated Fontina cheese
2 oz (50 g) freshly grated Pecorino cheese
3 eggs, lightly beaten
Salt
Freshly ground black pepper
13 oz (375 g) dried tortiglioni

◆

METHOD

Soak the ceps in warm water for 20 minutes. Drain them, retaining the strained soaking water. Squeeze the ceps dry and finely chop them.

Heat the oil and gently fry the button mushrooms. Add the ceps with 2–3 tablespoons soaking water and cook for about 5 minutes. Remove from the heat and gently stir in the ricotta, Fontina and Pecorino cheeses, and the beaten eggs. (The eggs should not be cooked; they should remain liquid at this stage.) Taste and add salt if necessary and pepper.

Meanwhile, cook the pasta for 6–7 minutes or until al dente, and drain. Return the pasta to the empty pan, and mix well with the sauce, so that the egg just starts to thicken with the heat of the pasta.

Gomiti alla Mozzarella

GOMITI WITH MOZZARELLA

Penne, farfalle or any other large pasta shapes or tubes would also be good with this sauce. The Campania region around the Bay of Naples is famous for its cooking cheese, Mozzarella, which makes a most mouthwatering sauce. This one is very simple to make.

SERVES 4

6 tablespoons olive oil
1 small onion, peeled and very finely chopped
1 × 14 oz (400 g) carton or bottle creamed or pulped tomatoes
5 basil leaves, shredded
Salt
13 oz (375 g) dried gomiti
11 oz (300 g) Mozzarella cheese, cut into very small cubes
2 oz (50 g) freshly grated Parmesan cheese
Freshly ground black pepper

METHOD

Heat the oil and fry the onion until golden. Add the tomatoes and the basil, cover and cook gently for 15 minutes. Add salt to taste.

Meanwhile, cook the pasta for 8–9 minutes or until al dente, and drain. Mix quickly with the Mozzarella cheese, the sauce and the Parmesan cheese, until the Mozzarella starts to melt with the heat of the pasta. Serve sprinkled with black pepper.

Rigatoni al ragù di maiale

RIGATONI WITH PORK RAGOUT

Rigatoni is another pasta which is very much loved in the south of Italy, where some people have it with hardly any sauce so they are able to taste the pasta itself.

A good ragout should cook for at least 1 hour. I remember my grandmother starting to prepare this sauce in the morning and letting it bubble away, just like hot volcanic lava, she used to say, until it was ready for lunch. By the way, the meat tastes heavenly at the end of the cooking. In Italy we would enjoy this dish with some vegetables as our main course.

SERVES 4

8 tablespoons olive oil

14 oz (400 g) pork with bone, e.g. neck, shoulder chops,
or spare ribs

1 onion, peeled and finely sliced

$^1/_4$ pint (150 ml) dry white wine

2 × 14 oz (400 g) cartons or bottles creamed or pulped tomatoes

2 tablespoons tomato purée

2 basil leaves, shredded

Salt

Freshly ground black pepper

13 oz (375 g) dried rigatoni

3 oz (75 g) freshly grated Parmesan cheese

METHOD

Heat the olive oil in a heavy-based saucepan, add the meat and fry for several minutes until browned. Add the onion and fry until golden. Pour in the wine and let the alcohol evaporate for 2 minutes. Add the tomatoes and the tomato purée, cover and simmer very gently for 30 minutes. Stir the contents from time to time. Add the basil, salt and black pepper to taste, and cook for another 30 minutes. If the sauce becomes too dry add a little water.

Meanwhile, cook the pasta for 8–9 minutes or until al dente, and drain. Mix the pasta with some of the sauce and serve with the remaining sauce and the Parmesan cheese.

Sedani con zucchini e noci

SEDANI WITH COURGETTES AND WALNUTS

This tubular pasta is named after the Italian for celery because it looks like a stem of celery: ribbed outside and hollow inside. This is one of my spontaneous sauces which came to my mind when I didn't have anything else in the house but the few ingredients listed below. This recipe demonstrates that pasta goes really well with anything, as long as you give it enough flavour.

SERVES 4

3 oz (75 g) butter
7 oz (200 g) leeks, trimmed and finely sliced
1 lb (450 g) courgettes, trimmed and very finely sliced
2 oz (50 g) walnut halves, roughly chopped
2 tablespoons chopped parsley
2 tablespoons chopped fresh coriander
Salt
Freshly ground black pepper
2–3 tablespoons milk
13 oz (375 g) dried sedani
3 oz (75 g) freshly grated Pecorino cheese

METHOD

Heat the butter and gently fry the leeks until golden. Add the courgettes and cook gently until very soft. Add the walnuts, parsley, coriander, and salt and pepper to taste. Stir in enough milk to loosen the consistency.

Cook the pasta for 8–9 minutes or until al dente, and drain. Mix with the sauce. Serve sprinkled with the Pecorino cheese.

Farfalle alla Fontina e porcini

---◆---

FARFALLE WITH FONTINA AND CEPS

The Fontina cheese, which comes from the Aosta Valley, bordering France and Switzerland, gives a wonderful creaminess to the dish without it being too cheesy or becoming lumpy. Cheese is always an important product of mountainous regions and two special breeds of cattle are reared to yield the milk for Fontina cheese. Imitations are not nearly as good as the genuine Fontina which states that it comes from the Val d'Aosta.

◆

SERVES 4

7 oz (200 g) fresh cep or shiitake mushrooms, sliced, or
³/₄ oz (20 g) dried ceps
3 oz (75 g) butter
1 small onion, peeled and finely chopped
1 × 14 oz (400 g) carton or bottle creamed or pulped tomatoes
6–8 basil leaves, chopped
13 oz (375 g) dried farfalle
7 oz (200 g) coarsely grated Fontina cheese
Salt
Freshly ground black pepper
3 oz (75 g) freshly grated Parmesan cheese

◆

METHOD

If using dried ceps soak them in warm water for 20 minutes. Drain the ceps and squeeze dry. Finely chop them.

Heat the butter and fry the onion until golden. Add the ceps (fresh or dried) or shiitake and fry them for 2 minutes. Stir in the tomatoes. Add the basil leaves and cook for another 5 minutes.

Meanwhile, cook the pasta for 8–9 minutes or until al dente. Add the Fontina cheese to the sauce, with salt and pepper to taste. If necessary gently heat the cheese through so that it melts before you toss the drained pasta with the sauce. Serve sprinkled with the Parmesan cheese.

Orecchiette al ragù di agnello

·

ORECCHIETTE WITH LAMB RAGOUT

This is a similar sauce to the basic ragù or Bolognese sauce (see page 45), only it contains more meat. Try to use neck cutlets of lamb for this sauce because they give it a fine flavour, and are ideal as a main course, after or alongside the pasta.

Orecchiette baresi are so called because they are originally from Bari in Puglia.

♦

SERVES 4

2 tablespoons olive oil

1¼ lb (550 g) neck cutlets of lamb

1 onion, peeled and finely sliced

¼ pint (150 ml) dry white wine

2 × 14 oz (400 g) cartons or bottles creamed or pulped tomatoes

1 tablespoon tomato purée

Salt

Freshly ground black pepper

14 oz (400 g) dried orecchiette baresi

3 oz (75 g) freshly grated Pecorino cheese

♦

METHOD

Heat the oil in a heavy-based pan and fry the lamb cutlets on both sides until browned. Add the onion and fry until soft. Add the wine and continue cooking for 2–3 minutes. Stir in the tomatoes and tomato purée, cover and simmer very gently for about 1 hour. Stir the contents from time to time. If the sauce becomes too dry add a little water. Add salt and pepper to taste.

Meanwhile, cook the pasta for 12–14 minutes or until al dente, and drain. Mix with the sauce. Serve sprinkled with the Pecorino cheese.

PASTA INCROSTATA (right)
See page 160
CANNOLICCHI AL FRESCO (left)
See page 161

Orecchioni piccanti

ORECCHIONI WITH PIQUANT SAUCE

Orecchiette baresi is a special pasta hand-made in the Puglia region. It is usually dressed with a meaty sauce (see page 45). For this rather giant version of the pasta, called orecchioni and looking like big ears, I developed this piquant sauce to make the pasta morsels even more interesting.

◆

SERVES 4

4 oz (100 g) sun-dried tomatoes
4 anchovy fillets (salted or in oil)
3 tablespoons coarsely chopped basil
3 tablespoons coarsely chopped parsley
$1/4$ oz (10 g) capers
2 cloves garlic, peeled and finely chopped
1 small chilli pepper
1 oz (25 g) stoned black olives
6 tablespoons virgin olive oil
$1/2$ pint (300 ml) water
12 oz (350 g) dried orecchioni
2 oz (50 g) freshly grated Pecorino cheese

◆

METHOD

Soak the sun-dried tomatoes in luke-warm water for about $1^{1}/_{2}$ hours until soft and the saltiness has been removed.

If using salted anchovies, also soak them in water for $1/2$ hour. Dry the anchovies on paper towels and remove any large bones. Drain the tomatoes and purée them in a food processor with 2 tablespoons each of the basil and parsley, the anchovies, capers, garlic, chilli pepper, olives, olive oil and water, until the mixture is smooth and glossy.

Cook the pasta for 20–25 minutes, or until al dente. Meanwhile, gently simmer the tomato mixture in a pan for 5 minutes, adding a little more water if becoming too thick. Drain the pasta and mix with the sauce.

Add the Pecorino cheese, mix together well and serve with the remaining basil and parsley sprinkled on top.

Pizzoccheri vegetariani

VEGETARIAN PIZZOCCHERI

Alta Valtellina, a valley in the northern part of Lombardy near the city of Sondrio, is the home of the famous bresaola, air-dried fillet of beef. It is also the home of pizzoccheri, a special pasta made from Italian 00 flour, buckwheat flour and durum wheat bran. Being so high in fibre, pizzoccheri is especially good for healthy eating, but unfortunately only a few very good food shops stock it. So, the moral to this tale is, buy more than you need when you do discover it!

♦

SERVES 6

12 oz (350 g) dried pizzoccheri
8 oz (225 g) potatoes, peeled and diced
7 oz (200 g) fresh French beans or spring greens or
Brussels sprouts, trimmed
5 oz (150 g) unsalted butter
2 cloves garlic, peeled and finely sliced
Freshly grated nutmeg
Few sage leaves, chopped
7 oz (200 g) Fontina cheese, diced
4 oz (100 g) freshly grated Parmesan cheese

♦

METHOD

Cook the pasta, potatoes and French beans, spring greens or Brussels sprouts together for 20–25 minutes or until tender. Drain the pasta and the vegetables.

Heat the butter and gently fry the garlic for a few minutes, adding the nutmeg and sage.

Preheat a large serving bowl. Put a layer of the pasta and the vegetables in the bottom, sprinkle with some of the Fontina cheese and some of the Parmesan cheese. Repeat the layers once again. Pour the hot butter, sage and garlic over the top, mix slightly into the pasta, and serve.

Insalate di Pasta e Riciclaggio Avanzi

PASTA SALADS AND TASTY LEFTOVERS

Pasta salads, which are usually prepared in the summer, lack the satisfying warmth of freshly cooked pasta. So the answer is to give the salad flavour and interest in a different and more decisive way. This doesn't mean overdoing the herbs and spices and I would certainly avoid mayonnaise in pasta salads as it generally makes the dish look less appetising. You need to achieve harmony of flavours compatible with the shape of the pasta (which is usually a short one).

An important part of Italian cookery is dedicated to using the leftovers of pasta which regularly occur more or less intentionally in every household! In some restaurants in Milan you can order a crusted pasta which is prepared with the pasta specially cooked and dressed beforehand to create this result.

*The best way to re-heat pasta is either in the oven or in a pan – **not** in a microwave! When re-heating it in the oven, cover the dish with foil to prevent the pasta becoming too dry; remove the foil for the last few minutes of re-heating to get a crisp crust. To re-heat pasta in a pan you usually need a little fat such as butter or olive oil together with some liquid which could be good stock or some leftover sauce or milk. Parmesan cheese, parsley, salt and pepper are also sometimes added.*

Frittata di maccheroni

◆

PASTA OMELETTE

There is no Pasquetta (Easter Monday) for many Italian families without a frittata di maccheroni. On this day, weather permitting, everybody takes this dish with them on a picnic, wherever they are – in the country, at the beach, or in the mountains. For me it brings back pleasurable childhood memories of days out-of-doors with my family.

◆

SERVES 4–6

6 tablespoons olive oil
1 quantity cooked Spaghettini al pomodoro e basilico (see page 124)
or Linguine al tonno (see page 133) or Maccheroncini alla
napoletana (see page 142)
2 oz (50 g) freshly grated Parmesan cheese
4 tablespoons finely chopped parsley
Salt
Freshly ground black pepper
6 eggs, lightly beaten

◆

METHOD

Heat half of the oil in a large, deep frying pan, add the pasta and heat thoroughly. Stir the Parmesan cheese, parsley, salt and pepper, and the beaten eggs into the pasta and fry gently until a crust forms on the bottom of the pasta. Invert the pasta omelette on to a plate and then put back in the pan, adding the remainder of the oil to cook the other side. Serve hot or cold.

Pasta incrostata

◆

PASTA WITH A CRUST

This is an ideal way to use one of my spaghetti recipes either cooked specially, or by making a larger quantity in the first place and making it last two days. The most important point is that you should use one of the long pastas like spaghetti, linguine or tagliatelle. These create the crust which holds the pasta together and is particularly tasty. You will need a very large frying pan so the pasta can be cooked in a thin layer.

◆

SERVES 4

2 oz (50 g) butter
1/2–3/4 quantity cooked Spaghettini al pomodoro e basilico
(see page 124)

◆

METHOD

Heat the butter in a very large frying pan. Add the pasta and without stirring cook it for 10 minutes or until a crust forms on the bottom. If you like the crust on both sides, as I do, follow the instructions for turning the pasta which are given in the previous recipe.

Cannolicchi al fresco

◆

PASTA SALAD AL FRESCO

This simple dish is just what you need on a hot sunny day.

◆

SERVES 4

4 tablespoons virgin olive oil
1 clove garlic, peeled and finely chopped
1 × 14 oz (400 g) tin chopped tomatoes
2 tablespoons finely chopped basil leaves
Salt
Freshly ground black pepper
11 oz (300 g) dried tubetti lisci

◆

METHOD

Heat the oil, add the garlic and fry until softened but not browned. Add the tomatoes, basil, and salt and pepper to taste, cover and cook for 10 minutes.

Meanwhile, cook the pasta for 8–9 minutes or until slightly softer than al dente, and drain. Mix with the sauce and eat at room temperature.

PASTA PER TUTTE LE STAGIONI
See page 169

Pasta fredda con vegetali

PASTA SALAD WITH VEGETABLES

This is great for parties but there's no reason not to prepare it just for yourself. I like to eat it either cold, or when the pasta is still slightly warm.

◆

SERVES 4

7 oz (200 g) fresh asparagus, trimmed

7 oz (200 g) celeriac, peeled and cut into large matchsticks

Salt

11 oz (300 g) dried gomiti

6 tablespoons virgin olive oil

2 tablespoons white wine vinegar

Freshly ground black pepper

2 very large tomatoes, peeled, de-seeded and roughly chopped

7 oz (200 g) Mozzarella cheese, diced

4 oz (100 g) Pecorino cheese, cut into strips

2 tablespoons finely chopped basil

◆

METHOD

Cook the asparagus and celeriac separately in slightly salted, boiling water until tender, allowing about 20 minutes. Drain and allow to cool. Cut the asparagus into 1 inch (2.5 cm) pieces.

Cook the pasta for 7 minutes or until slightly softer than al dente. Drain and allow to cool slightly.

In a bowl mix together the oil, vinegar, salt and pepper. Stir in the tomatoes, Mozzarella and Pecorino cheeses, celeriac, asparagus and basil. Mix well. Add the pasta, stir well and taste again for seasoning. Serve cold or slightly warm.

Pasta fredda con pesce

PASTA SALAD WITH FISH

Often you can make pasta salads with leftovers but for this recipe it is much better to make it fresh so the flavour and texture of the fish do not suffer.

◆

SERVES 4

10 anchovy fillets (salted or in oil)
11 oz (300 g) medium-sized dried farfalle or conchiglie
7 oz (200 g) squid, cleaned and cut into strips
Salt
6 tablespoons virgin olive oil
Juice of 1 lemon
Freshly ground black pepper
4 oz (100 g) smoked salmon, cut into strips
7 oz (200 g) peeled, small, cooked prawns (fresh or frozen)
3 tablespoons finely chopped chives
3 tablespoons finely chopped dill

◆

METHOD

If using salted anchovies soak them in water for ½ hour. Dry them on paper towels and remove any large bones. Cut them into pieces.

Cook the pasta for 7 minutes or until slightly softer than al dente. Drain and allow to cool.

Cook the squid in salted, boiling water for 5 minutes. Drain and cool.

In a bowl mix together the oil, lemon juice, salt and pepper. Add the cooked squid, the smoked salmon, anchovies, prawns, chives and dill, and mix well. Add the pasta, stir well and taste again for seasoning. Serve cold.

ZITI AL FORNO ALLA NAPOLETANA
See page 176

Pasta fredda con carne

PASTA SALAD WITH MEAT

Ideally some leftovers of roast duck or turkey would do very nicely here but you can use roast beef or chicken instead.

♦

SERVES 4

11 oz (300 g) dried pennette lisce
4 oz (100 g) smoked lean bacon, rinded and cut into pieces
6 tablespoons virgin olive oil
2 tablespoons tarragon vinegar or white wine vinegar
Salt
Freshly ground black pepper
7 oz (200 g) roast duck (preferably breast), cut into strips
4 oz (100 g) Mozzarella cheese, cut into narrow strips
4 oz (100 g) lean Parma ham
1–2 tablespoons finely chopped parsley
2 tablespoons finely chopped spring onions
2 large gherkins pickled with dill, cut into matchsticks
1 tablespoon creamed horseradish
Few drops Tabasco sauce

♦

METHOD

Cook the pasta for 7 minutes or until slightly softer than al dente. Drain and allow to cool. Fry the bacon in its own fat until crisp and drain on paper towels.

Put the oil, vinegar, salt and pepper in a bowl and mix well. Add all the other ingredients and mix together well with the pasta. Taste again for seasoning. Serve cold.

Pasta per tutte le stagioni

◆

PASTA FOR ALL SEASONS

To complete this chapter I couldn't go without giving you a recipe involving my beloved ingredient – mushrooms. It also includes truffle oil, a very sophisticated and, unfortunately, expensive item which is available in good delicatessens and Italian food shops. This is a dish for special occasions, and can be eaten warm or cold.

◆

SERVES 4

5 oz (150 g) fresh shiitake mushrooms
5 oz (150 g) fresh oyster mushrooms
4 oz (100 g) chanterelles
6 tablespoons olive oil
1 small garlic clove, peeled and finely chopped
2 tablespoons finely chopped parsley
Salt
Freshly ground black pepper
Juice of 1 lemon
11 oz (300 g) small dried fusilli
5 oz (150 g) smoked ham, cut into small strips
3 tablespoons double cream (if you eat the dish warm)
2 tablespoons truffle oil and/or truffle

◆

METHOD

Clean the shiitake, oyster and chanterelle mushrooms and cut away the tough part of the stalk of the shiitake mushrooms. Cut the oyster and shiitake mushrooms into fine strips or use them whole if they are small.

Heat 4 tablespoons of the oil and fry the oyster and shiitake mushrooms. Add the chanterelles after a few minutes and continue to fry for another few minutes. Add the garlic, parsley, salt and pepper. Fry for another few minutes, then add the lemon juice. Mix well and set aside.

Cook the pasta for 8–9 minutes or until slightly softer than al dente. Drain and mix in a bowl with the ham and the mushroom mixture, and add the cream if you are eating the dish warm. Sprinkle with the truffle oil before serving. Slices of truffle added to this dish make it very, very special.

Timballi di Pasta

PASTA TIMBALES

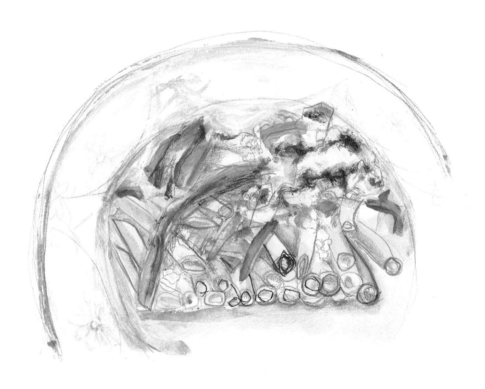

You may wonder why we should make a timbale, when all the ingredients cooked for the first stage of the dish would be good enough to eat as they are! The answer is that the timbale produces a richer, more opulent dish, which is just what you need when all the family or many friends are gathered together. The extra effort completely justifies the results which will please everybody. The preparation will please you, in particular, because the perfect place to finish a timbale is in the oven, so you have time to join in the fun. Whilst the layers stay soft and moist a fantastic crispness develops on top – it has to be tasted to be believed.

Rigatoni alla ricca bolognese

RIGATONI WITH RICH BOLOGNESE SAUCE

Bologna la Ricca they say in Italy, referring to the rich city. In Bologna the food is usually rich too, and this dish is a fine example of the local cuisine. You can prepare the dish a day in advance, let it set for 24 hours and bake it at the last minute, leaving you time for your guests. You need at least 5 or 6 friends with healthy appetites to share the meal.

◆

SERVES 5–6

7 oz (200 g) fresh ceps, finely sliced, or 7 oz (200 g) button
mushrooms, finely sliced, together with
$^3/_4$ oz (20 g) dried ceps
5 oz (150 g) veal sweetbreads, cleaned
6 tablespoons olive oil
1 onion, peeled and finely chopped
7 oz (200 g) chicken livers, cut into small pieces
7 oz (200 g) chicken breasts or veal, coarsely minced
4 oz (100 g) lean Parma ham, thickly sliced and cut into strips
$^1/_4$ pint (150 ml) dry Marsala wine
3 × 1 lb (450 g) cartons or bottles creamed or pulped tomatoes
Salt
Freshly ground black pepper
$1^3/_4$ pints (1 litre) milk
2 oz (50 g) butter
2 tablespoons plain flour
Freshly grated nutmeg
1 lb (450 g) dried rigatoni
5 oz (150 g) freshly grated Parmesan cheese

◆

METHOD

Pre-heat the oven to 220°C/425°C/gas mark 7.

If using dried ceps, soak them in warm water for 20 minutes. Drain the ceps and squeeze dry, then roughly chop them.

Put the sweetbreads in boiling water and blanch for 10 minutes. Strain and remove the skin and nerves. Slice the sweetbreads.

To make the meat sauce: heat the oil in a large, heavy-based pan and fry the onion for 1 minute. Add the chicken livers, minced chicken or veal and Parma ham, and fry for another few minutes. Add the sweetbreads and continue to fry until everything is lightly browned. Add the fresh ceps, or the button mushrooms and dried ceps, to the pan, with the Marsala wine. Simmer gently for about 2 minutes, then stir in the tomatoes. Cover and simmer the sauce very gently for 2 hours, stirring from time to time. Taste and add salt and pepper.

To make the white sauce: bring the milk to the boil in a saucepan. In a separate pan melt the butter and stir in the flour. Cook the butter and flour for 1 minute over a moderate heat, stirring continuously, to make a roux. Reduce the heat and gradually stir in the milk until the sauce has thickened. Add salt and nutmeg to taste and set aside.

Cook the pasta for just 4 minutes, and drain. Toss in a little of the white sauce to prevent the pasta shapes from sticking together.

Lightly butter an 8 × 10 inch (20 × 25 cm) baking dish with sides about 3 inches (7.5 cm) deep. Put a layer of pasta in the dish, then add one-third of the meat sauce, followed by one-third of the white sauce. Sprinkle with Parmesan cheese. Repeat this sequence twice more, finishing with Parmesan cheese. Bake for 40 minutes.

TORTELLINI IN SARCOFAGO
See page 178

Ziti al forno alla Napoletana

ZITI NEAPOLITAN-STYLE

Ziti, zita or zite is a sort of long tubular noodle for everyday eating, served with just a tomato sauce and perhaps some small cubes of Mozzarella cheese. But it is also something we use for grand occasions. Then we create a dish like this one here, which is very rich and you really only need a little square to be satisfied. This recipe takes some time and patience, but the result makes it worthwhile. Let me show you how my mother taught me to cook it.

♦

SERVES 8

FOR THE MEATBALLS

11 oz (300 g) minced beef

1 clove garlic, peeled and finely chopped

1 tablespoon chopped parsley

1 oz (25 g) freshly grated Parmesan cheese

2 eggs, lightly beaten

1½ oz (40 g) fresh breadcrumbs, soaked in a little milk
for 5 minutes, then squeezed dry

Salt

Freshly ground black pepper

Oil, for frying

FOR THE SAUCE

4 tablespoons olive oil

1 onion, peeled and chopped

4 oz (100 g) chicken livers, chopped

2 × 14 oz (400 g) tins chopped tomatoes

5 basil leaves, shredded

FOR THE LAYERS

1 lb (450 g) dried ziti

4 oz (100 g) spicy Neapolitan salami, sliced

12 oz (350 g) Fontina or good Mozzarella cheese

4 eggs, lightly beaten

3 oz (75 g) freshly grated Parmesan cheese

♦

METHOD

Pre-heat the oven to 200°C/400°F/gas mark 6.

To make the meatballs: mix together the minced beef, the garlic, parsley, Parmesan cheese, eggs and breadcrumbs in a bowl. Add salt and pepper and mix thoroughly. Use your hands to shape the mixture into walnut-sized meatballs.

Heat a little oil in a frying pan and fry the meatballs in batches for about 3 minutes until browned on all sides. Remove and drain on paper towels.

To make the sauce: heat the oil in a clean pan and fry the onion until nearly transparent. Add the chicken livers and cook for another 3 minutes. Stir in the tomatoes, cover and simmer for 20 minutes over a low heat. Add the basil, salt and pepper, and simmer for another 10 minutes.

Meanwhile, cook the pasta for 5–7 minutes or until al dente, and drain. Toss with some of the sauce so that the pasta is coated.

Lightly butter an 8 × 10 inch (20 × 25 cm) baking dish with sides 3 inches (7.5 cm) deep. Spread a layer of sauce over the bottom, then add a layer of pasta. Arrange some salami, some of the meatballs and slices of Fontina or Mozzarella cheese on top. Repeat this sequence until all the ingredients are used. When you reach the final layer of Fontina or Mozzarella cheese, pour on the beaten eggs which will bind the pasta together. Finish with a layer of sauce and the Parmesan cheese.

Bake for 25 minutes. When it is cooked let the dish stand for 5 minutes before dividing it into portions with a knife and serving.

Tortellini in sarcofago

·

TORTELLINI IN SARCOFAGO

The idea of putting pasta in a pastry case is to collect all the aromas and to release them at once in front of the guests. One could also say it is a good piece of culinary showmanship! In any case your guests will react with surprise and admiration.

◆

SERVES 4

14 oz (400 g) frozen puff pastry, thawed
1½ oz (40 g) butter, plus extra for greasing
1 small shallot, peeled and finely chopped
4 oz (100 g) cooked smoked ham
4 leaves sage
A little freshly grated nutmeg
14 oz (400 g) fresh, meat-filled tortellini
7 fl oz (200 ml) single cream
3 oz (75 g) freshly grated Parmesan cheese
Salt
Freshly ground black pepper
A little milk

◆

METHOD

Pre-heat the oven to 220°C/425°F/gas mark 7.

On a lightly floured surface roll out the puff pastry thinly until it is large enough to cover the back of an ovenproof oval saucepan or baking dish, approximately 9 × 7 inches (23 × 18 cm) and 3 inches (7.5 cm) deep.

Cut out the pastry round the saucepan or baking dish base, allowing an extra 3 inches (7.5 cm) all round, and also cut out a lid, slightly larger than the base of the saucepan or dish.

Lightly butter the back of the saucepan or dish and with the help of the rolling pin shape the larger piece of pastry over it. Trim the edges to neaten.

Lightly butter a baking tray to take the pastry lid. Bake both base and lid for 25–30 minutes until golden. Allow to cool slightly before removing the pastry base and carefully place it on an ovenproof serving dish.

Heat the 1¹/₂ oz (40 g) butter in a pan and briefly fry the shallot for 1 minute. Add the ham, sage and nutmeg and continue frying for another 2 minutes, stirring.

Meanwhile cook the pasta for 3 minutes and drain. Add the cream, Parmesan cheese and pasta to the ham mixture and mix well. Add seasoning to taste. Pour the mixture into the pastry base. Cover lightly with the lid and brush the top with milk. Bake for 5 minutes to reheat the pastry, and serve at once.

Tullgarnspaj

TULLGARN'S PIE

Some Swedish friends, Count and Countess Bernadotte, have passed me an interesting recipe which, in times of general concern about healthy diet, falls like a bombshell. It is interesting because it includes spaghetti and Parmesan cheese, Italian influences picked up during visits to Italy by the Swedish royal family. This is King Gustav V's special picnic dish; it was developed under the instruction of Princess Victoria by the chefs of Tullgarn – a summer residence of the royal family. The filling can be varied with veal, pork, beef, game or poultry.

It is not an enclosed pie, but it has a base and crust of puff pastry and cooks to a fairly firm dish. It is very rich so should be served in small quantities.

◆

SERVES 12–16

5 oz (150 g) puff pastry made with butter
9 oz (250 g) veal sweetbreads, soaked for 2 hours
1¹/₄ pints (700 ml) double cream
¹/₄ pint (150 ml) beef stock
Salt
Freshly ground black pepper
14 oz (400 g) dried spaghetti
7 oz (200 g) butter, melted
Pinch of freshly grated nutmeg
2 eggs and 1 egg yolk
5 oz (150 g) freshly grated Parmesan cheese
5 oz (150 g) cooked salt beef, finely chopped
7 oz (200 g) cooked chicken, cubed
1–2 tomatoes, skinned and sliced

◆

Pre-heat the oven to 200°C/400°F/gas mark 6 and lightly butter an 8 inch (20 cm) soufflé dish with 6 inch (15 cm) deep sides.

Divide the pastry in half, roll out one half on a lightly floured surface and use to line the base of the dish.

Drain the sweetbreads and place in a pan of cold water. Bring to the boil, simmer for 5 minutes, then drain. Pull away the ducts, remove the skin and some of the outer membrane, but not too much or the sweetbreads will break up during cooking. Place in a pan with 4 tablespoons of the double cream and the beef stock, bring to the boil, then simmer gently for 15 minutes. Remove the sweetbreads from the pan and slice thickly.

Bring a large saucepan of salted water to the boil, add the spaghetti, bring back to the boil and boil for 4 minutes. Drain well, return to the hot pan and add 14 fl oz (500 ml) of the cream and 4 oz (100 g) of the melted butter. Season generously with salt, pepper and nutmeg and stir over a gentle heat.

Meanwhile, beat the whole eggs with the remaining cream.

Arrange a little spaghetti on the pastry in the base of the dish, sprinkle with Parmesan and add layers of salt beef, egg mixture, sweetbreads and the remaining melted butter. Continue layering until all the ingredients have been used up, finishing with pasta and Parmesan. Top with the chicken and tomatoes. Roll out the remaining pastry and use to cover the top. Brush with the egg yolk and bake in the oven for 30 minutes until golden brown.

Timballo di penne con melanzane e Mozzarella

TIMBALLO DI PENNE WITH AUBERGINES AND SMOKED MOZZARELLA CHEESE

In Italy the combination of pasta and vegetables has always been made interesting with no-one missing, or even thinking it should contain, meat. This is a good example. Again it's a recipe worth cooking for several people. Serve with a salad and a good Soave wine.

♦

SERVES 6-8

1 lb (450 g) dried penne lisce
1¹/₂ oz (40 g) butter, cut into pieces
7 oz (200 g) French beans, fresh or frozen
2 tablespoons olive oil
1 lb (450 g) carrots, peeled and cut into large matchsticks
2 large aubergines, peeled and cut lengthwise into
¹/₂ inch (1 cm) strips
1 small clove garlic, peeled and finely chopped
Pinch of freshly grated nutmeg
Salt
Freshly ground black pepper
2 × 11 oz (300 g) smoked Mozzarella cheese, cut into strips
14 oz (400 g) ricotta cheese
5 oz (150 g) freshly grated Parmesan cheese
8 eggs, lightly beaten

♦

METHOD

Pre-heat the oven to 200°C/400°F/gas mark 6.

Cook the pasta for 5–6 minutes or until al dente, and drain. Mix the pasta with the butter and set aside.

Cook the French beans in water until tender. Drain and set aside.

Heat the oil and fry the carrots until lightly browned on all sides. Add the aubergines and the garlic, and fry until golden. Add a pinch of nutmeg, and salt and pepper.

Lightly butter an 8 × 10 inch (20 × 25 cm) baking dish with sides 3 inches (7.5 cm) deep. Cover the bottom with a third of the cooked pasta. Put one-third of the beans, carrots, aubergines, Mozzarella cheese and ricotta cheese over the pasta, and sprinkle with Parmesan cheese. Repeat this sequence twice more, finishing with Parmesan cheese. Pour on the beaten eggs, which will bind the pasta together. Bake for 30 minutes.

Pasta da Dessert

PASTA PUDDINGS

If you think of that British favourite, bread and butter pudding, then the idea that pasta can be eaten as a pudding won't seem so remarkable. Pasta, like bread, consists of flour and water. Add sugar and some other interesting ingredients and the unexpected becomes irresistible! Pasta fanatics like eating pasta in any form; perhaps after this chapter you will too.

Torta di Zia Dora

AUNT DORA TART

While my mother had plenty to do in raising my four elder brothers and sisters, as the youngest I was privileged to spend my holidays with my Aunt Dora, near Avellino (just east of Naples) in a charming little village called Prata. I have the most beautiful memories from this time, one of which is of this cake which was prepared by her domestic helper, Lina. After 45 years Lina still lives with my Aunt, and for me her recipe is unforgettable.

Cedro is better than candied lemon peel for this, so try to get it from a delicatessen or Italian food shop, if you possibly can. My serving suggestion is to drink a glass of a Lacrima Christi wine (or a sweet sherry) with this tart.

◆

SERVES 4

7 oz (200 g) dried linguine

1 oz (25 g) butter

10 eggs, lightly beaten

7 oz (200 g) vanilla sugar (see opposite)

Seeds from a vanilla pod, crushed

1 teaspoon Strega liqueur

4 oz (100 g) cedro, or candied lemon peel, chopped

1 teaspoon ground cinnamon

4 oz (100 g) glacé cherries, halved

4 oz (100 g) bitter dark chocolate, broken into small cubes

◆

METHOD

Pre-heat the oven to 150°C/300°F/gas mark 2.

Cook the pasta for 8 minutes or until slightly softer than al dente. Drain and allow to cool.

Beat together the butter, eggs, vanilla sugar, vanilla seeds and the Strega liqueur. Stir the cedro or candied lemon peel, cinnamon, cherries and the chocolate into the egg mixture. Add the pasta and mix well.

Pour the mixture into a well greased, large baking dish or flan tin. Bake for 30 minutes.

Fettuccine al papavero

·

FETTUCCINE WITH POPPY SEEDS

From my student times spent in Vienna one of the most memorable desserts was a Moonnudeln or poppy pasta. I made my own adaptation to create this recipe which I believe has Bohemian origins.

◆

SERVES 4

1 oz (25 g) black poppy seeds
7 oz (200 g) pappardelle or tagliatelle
3 oz (75 g) unsalted butter
$^1/_2$ tablespoon freshly grated nutmeg
$^1/_4$ tablespoon ground cloves
Pinch of freshly ground black pepper
3 oz (75 g) vanilla sugar (see below),
or caster sugar and vanilla essence to taste

◆

METHOD

Roast the poppy seeds in a very hot oven for 10 minutes. Cook the pasta in unsalted water until al dente. Heat the butter in a pan and add the poppy seeds and spices. Add vanilla essence to taste if not using vanilla sugar. Drain the pasta, divide between four plates and sprinkle with the vanilla sugar or caster sugar.

Zucchero vanigliato

·

VANILLA SUGAR

Vanilla sugar is simply made by putting one or two vanilla pods, cut into pieces, into a jar of caster sugar. Leave 2–3 weeks. You can go on re-filling the jar with sugar, using the same vanilla pods for many months.

PASTA AL CIOCCOLATO (right)
See page 189
FUTTUCCINE AL PAPAVERO (left)
See page 185

Fettuccine dolci

SWEET FETTUCCINE

This is based on an extremely simple pastry, which everyone can make. We make this pastry all over Italy; giving it a different name according to the region, town and even village! Its only drawback is that the dough has to rest for a couple of hours, so you'll need to plan a bit ahead.

◆

SERVES 4

9 oz (250 g) plain flour
2 oz (50 g) butter, cut into pieces
1 large egg, lightly beaten
2 tablespoons granulated sugar
Pinch of salt
5 tablespoons sweet vermouth
Pork lard or dripping, for deep frying
Icing sugar

◆

METHOD

Sift the flour into a bowl and rub in the butter until the mixture resembles fine breadcrumbs. Add the egg, sugar, salt and finally the vermouth. Mix with a round-bladed knife to bring the mixture together, then knead for about 5 minutes until a smooth, fairly stiff dough is formed. Cover and leave the dough to rest in a cool place for at least 2 hours.

To make the ribbons, roll out the dough until ⅛ inch (3 mm) thick. With a pastry wheel, cut the dough into strips 1 inch (2.5 cm) wide and 8 inches (20 cm) long. Gently tie the strips into single bows. (If you have a pasta machine, you can use it to roll the dough out into the long strips.)

Heat the lard or dripping in a large, deep pan and when the fat is very hot, deep fry the bows 2 or 3 at a time until golden brown. Remove the bows, drain on paper towels and allow to cool. Make a mound of bows on a plate and serve sprinkled with icing sugar.

Pasta al cioccolato

•

CHOCOLATE PASTA

In Italy there already exists a type of chocolate pasta, which is made with very bitter chocolate and is usually served with game sauce. This recipe was developed in the Neal Street Kitchens and is dedicated to all chocoholics!

•

SERVES 4

FOR THE PASTA
9 oz (250 g) plain flour
4 oz (100 g) cocoa powder
1 oz (25 g) caster sugar
Pinch of cinnamon
4 eggs
$^1/_2$ teaspoon vanilla essence

FOR THE SAUCE
4 teaspoons good-quality clear honey
4 tablespoons chopped pistachio nuts

♦

METHOD

Sift the flour with the cocoa powder, and stir in the sugar and cinnamon. Make a well in the centre of the dry ingredients and add the eggs and vanilla essence, and mix to a smooth dough.

Roll out the dough on a floured surface until $^1/_8$ inch (3 mm) thick. With a pastry wheel cut the dough into strips $^3/_4$ inch (2 cm) wide and about 7 inches (18 cm) long. (If you have a pasta machine, you can use it to roll the dough out into the ribbons.)

Cook the pasta in unsalted, boiling water for 3 minutes. Drain and divide between 4 warmed plates. Drizzle a generous teaspoon of honey and sprinkle 1 tablespoon pistachio nuts over each serving.

INDEX

———— ♦ ————

Page numbers in *italic* refer to photographs